_An_
EDWARDIAN
CHILDHOOD

An EDWARDIAN CHILDHOOD

JANE PETTIGREW

A BULFINCH PRESS BOOK
LITTLE, BROWN AND COMPANY
BOSTON · TORONTO · LONDON

For Richard and Nicholas

Acknowledgements

The author would like to express very warm thanks to Madge
Hodson for the fascinating stories of her childhood; to Maria
Leach at Little, Brown for her very kind and patient guidance; to
Julie Anne Wilson at the Bodleian Library for her untiring efforts
to find suitable illustrations and to Pamela Norris for her
generous and expert advice.

Text and compilation copyright © 1991 by Jane Pettigrew

First North American Edition 1992
First published in Great Britain in 1991 by
Little, Brown and Company (UK) Limited

ISBN 0-8212-1915-4
Library of Congress Cataloging-in-Publication information is available.

Designed by Janet James

Bulfinch Press is an imprint and trademark
of Little, Brown and Company (Inc.)
Published simultaneously in Canada by
Little, Brown & Company (Canada) Limited

PRINTED IN ITALY

CONTENTS

INTRODUCTION

Queen Victoria's death on 22 January 1901 marked the start of the new century and a turning-point for Britain. Nineteenth-century imperialism, growth and optimism were to give way slowly to decline and gloomy pessimism about Britain's place in the world and her future political and economic capabilities. King Edward ruled for a ten-year period of great restlessness and change, when rich people grew richer than ever before but millions still lived in poverty. Of a population in 1900 of thirty-seven million, twenty-seven million were working class, earning between ten and fifteen shillings a week from manual labour. The Liberal governments of 1905–14 put in place a number of reforms to ease the plight of the poor, but change was slow and the wealthy minority continued to enjoy a life of extravagant pleasure and easy comfort. The King, with his love of the good life, hunting, shooting, fishing, sailing and socializing, gave a somewhat stylish character to the period, and rich aristocrats and nouveau-riche industrialists and bankers liked to emulate his lifestyle and aspired constantly to greater wealth. Virginia Cowles writes: 'His pleasures were the pleasures of the senses – food, women, magnificence, and above all else, comfort. He had indulged his tastes for forty years, but his appetite was still unsatisfied. As a result the Edwardian era

Fun for everyone at a lively children's party.

sprang into being.' For the King and his circle, the social year was dominated by the London 'Season', that ran from May to August and brought floods of rich and powerful people to the capital 'City of Pleasure' for a continual round of receptions, balls, concerts, garden parties, dinners and dances, cricket matches, racing events and regattas.

But major changes in society were beginning to undermine and unsettle the wealth and stability

A bowl of soapy water amused small children for hours.

King Edward VII with his son Prince Edward of Cornwall and York, 1901.

that this rich minority liked to believe was still theirs. Tax laws were changing to the disadvantage of the very wealthy, trades unions were growing in power, the women's suffrage movement was taking hold and the middle classes were growing and encroaching on the strongholds of the upper classes. J.B. Priestley wrote in *The Edwardians* 'There was a vague feeling that the end was almost in sight, that their class was now banging away in the last act.' The Edwardian age was once described as a short-lived wedding party that lasted one brief decade. Virginia Cowles expands on this: 'Everything was larger than life-size. There was an avalanche of balls and dinners and country house parties. More money was spent on clothes, more food was consumed, more horses were raced ... more yachts were commissioned, more late hours were kept than ever before. It was, in short the most ostentatious and extravagant decade that England had known.' In fact, although the King died in 1910, the Edwardian period refers to the years leading up to the beginning of the First World War in 1914, by which time life was changing for everybody, rich and poor, in Britain.

The children of this 'Golden Age' benefited from a marked change in attitude from the harshness of Victorian days. Victorian children had always been treated as small adults and expected to behave similarly. Working-class children had always contributed to the family income by working in mines, factories and mills. Now, the

Edwardians showed more understanding of children's needs, and emphasized the joy and innocence of childhood. Politicians showed concern for children's welfare, and introduced measures to restrict and regulate the employment of minors, to reorganize and improve educational systems, to increase medical care, to provide free school meals to feed the poor and hungry, to clear slums and build new and better housing, and to protect junior miscreants from being treated as hardened criminals. The voice of social conscience expressed a great indignation against the rich and urged reforms that would benefit adults and children alike. In a period that saw the first motor cars, electric trams, trains and underground railways, the first aeroplanes, gas and electricity in the home, refrigeration, escalators, the opening up of the big stores, improvements in housing, health and education and the introduction of the vote for women, those demands for a fairer society helped to diminish the enormous gap between rich and poor and enabled the majority of children to take advantage of the improvements and innovations of the Edwardian age.

Singing games were very popular in school playground, street or meadow.

A CHILD'S PLACE

Children growing up in the first fourteen years of this century experienced life in as many different ways and circumstances as at any other time in British history. There were poor country children in humble village cottages; there were rich children in comfortable country houses; there were poor city children in urban slums; there were wealthy families in smart town villas; and there were very rich children from aristocratic families who spent part of their year in huge stately homes that stood in vast estates, and the other part, usually the summer months of the London Season, in expensive London mansions.

Rural children of all classes enjoyed the peace and quiet of an environment untouched by industrial noise and dirt. Poor children may not have had the luxury of large houses or servants, but they usually had enough to eat, were well cared for and enjoyed the simple pleasures of the countryside. Flora Thompson's Lark Rise did not change very much between the 1880s of her childhood and the early part of this century. 'Lark Rise,' she said, 'must not be thought of as a slum set down in the country. The inhabitants lived an open-air life: the cottages were kept clean by much scrubbing with

soap and water, and doors and windows stood wide open when the weather permitted. . . . In nearly all the cottages there was but one room downstairs, and many of these were poor and bare,

No matter how simple the setting, a tea party was always fun.

Children from all social backgrounds enjoyed the fresh air of the countryside.

with only a table and a few chairs and stools for furniture and a superannuated potato-sack thrown down by way of hearthrug. Other rooms were bright and cosy, with dressers of crockery, cushioned chairs, pictures on the walls and brightly coloured hand-made rag rugs on the floor. . . .' The children in such communities 'were taught good manners and taken for walks, milk was bought for them, and they were bathed regularly on Saturday nights and, after "Gentle Jesus" was said, were tucked into bed. . . .'

Poor city children were not so lucky. Their living conditions were often squalid, as Thomas Morgan, who lived in Blackfriars Road in London, recalls: 'We nearly always had one room, one used to have a sheet on the line to separate one room – make two of it. Us children slept one side and father and mother the other side.' Children were expected, at a very early age, to add to the family income by running paper rounds or delivering the milk before dashing off to school. Their playground was the street, their feet were often bare and their ragged clothes were hand-me-downs from parents or older brothers and sisters. But, with increasing job opportunities and regular wages some working-class families found that they could now afford to move out of the working class and its slums, into the growing middle class with its newly-built, neat and clean terraced properties in the expanding suburbs. A skilled or semi-skilled craftsman could afford the weekly rent of 12s 6d (62 pence today) on a solid five or

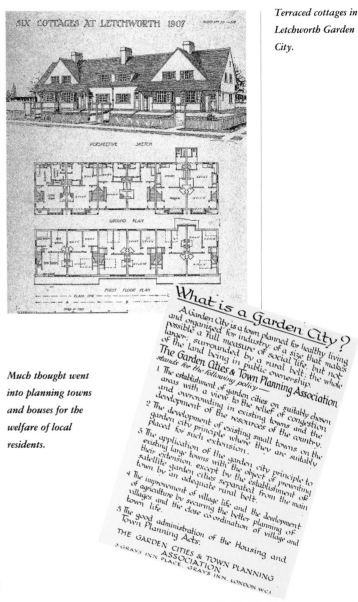

Terraced cottages in Letchworth Garden City.

Much thought went into planning towns and houses for the welfare of local residents.

What is a Garden City?

A Garden City is a town planned for healthy living and organized for industry: of a size that makes possible a full measure of social life, but not larger; surrounded by a rural belt; the whole of the land being in public ownership.

The Garden Cities & Town Planning Association stands for the following policy—

1 The establishment of garden cities on suitably chosen areas and with a view to the relief of congestion and overcrowding in existing towns and the development of the resources of the country.

2 The development of existing small towns on the garden city principle where they are suitably placed for such extension.

3 The application of the garden city principle to existing large towns with the object of preventing their extension, except by the establishment of satellite garden cities separated from the main town by an adequate rural belt.

4 The improvement of village life and the development of agriculture by securing the better planning of villages and the close co-ordination of village and town life.

5 The good administration of the Housing and Town Planning Acts.

THE GARDEN CITIES & TOWN PLANNING ASSOCIATION
3 GRAYS INN PLACE, GRAYS INN, LONDON WC1

six-roomed terraced house that was fitted with gas or oil lighting and was large enough to allow the family to rent one room out to a lodger, and keep the front room for only special occasions. In his autobiography Neville Cardus recalls his childhood house in Manchester where 'the living-room was the one used every day and we called it the kitchen. The front room or parlour, which enjoyed the bay windows, was occupied only on Sundays.' Food preparation and dish washing were done in a little scullery, and the family ate and spent most of its time together in the warm kitchen with its coal burner, sink, mangle for the washing and galvanized tin bath. Since there was no bathroom, baths were taken in front of the kitchen stove or fire, and washstands in each bedroom provided adequate facilities for daily washing. A small garden grew a few vegetables and allowed the children some space for games in the open air.

Similar simple but comfortable houses were constructed in the new towns at Bournville, built near Birmingham by the Cadbury family in 1878, and Port Sunlight, built by the Lever brothers on Merseyside in 1887. Town planning was a new phrase in Edwardian language, and Members of Parliament, local councillors and architects recognized the need for a cleaner environment, more space, gardens, playing fields, improved domestic facilities and community services as well as a social structure that allowed residents to feel that they belonged to a community. Letchworth Garden City was built in 1903, Rowntree Village Trust

was set up in 1904, and Hampstead Garden Suburb in 1907. Children who grew up in such 'modern' settings played outside in family gardens, communal playgrounds and sports fields, and enjoyed, like their parents, clean air, clean streets and warm, well-lit houses.

A Houseful of Servants

For upper-middle-class families, higher salaries bought grand three- or four-storey houses in select suburbs. These residences, with their fancy decoration, stone lintels over the windows and elegant fanlights, housed not just the family but a troupe of servants who cleaned, cooked, washed, ironed and looked after the children. More modest families usually employed at least one maid, but these wealthy households included anything up to

A typical surburban semi-detached house offered for sale in 1910 at £10 down and 10s 7d a week for 15 years.

ten servants. Very wealthy, upper-middle-class families moved out beyond the edges of the towns and settled in small county towns where life was elegant and refined and the children could play with suitable friends in large gardens.

The rich children of aristocratic and upper-class families lived on their fathers' country estates surrounded by nannies, maids, butlers, footmen, cooks, housekeepers and gardeners who ran the house and grounds and made sure that everyone had everything they wanted. Vita Sackville-West describes in her novel *The Edwardians* '... the loose and lavish extravagance' on which such houses were run. 'Everybody ... obtained exactly what they wanted; they had only to ask, and the request was fulfilled as though by magic. The

Wealthy London children could play in the elegant private gardens of the square.

house was really as self-contained as a little town; the carpenter's shop, the painter's shop, the forge, the sawmill, the hot-houses, were there to provide whatever might be needed at a moment's notice.'

The town houses where the families spent the Season were in the smarter parts of town where private gardens in elegant squares were kept locked against non-residents and front doors were opened by liveried footmen. Cynthia Asquith '. . . thought the Park tedious. What I loved was romping in the communal garden to which every householder in Cadogan Square had a key. Unless some special engagement forbade, I enjoyed this every evening after tea, and it was the one great redeeming feature of my London routine.' These town residences were often supplied with food and flowers from the country estate, so that all the familiar luxuries were available to the family and its guests, and necessary servants accompanied the family from country seat to urban mansion.

In a Child's World
In spite of the many different experiences of childhood resulting from these various situations, the patterns which emerge from personal recollections, biographies and social comment from the period suggest that on certain levels the lives of Edwardian children from all classes were very similar. These patterns, of course, depended on class and wealth, environment and the local community, family attitudes and religion. Individual experiences were further affected by each child's gender, position in the family and relationship with brothers and sisters, parents and servants. The pattern that emerges most strongly is in the lives of wealthy children whose parents understood the innocence and joy of childhood and wished to protect their infants from the worries and concerns of the adult world. Those privileged lives were safe and calm, healthy and comfortable, full of amusements, treats and distractions, and brightened by colourful toys and books. Their parents' desire to provide a sheltered, stable environment led to the children having their own closeted world away from the rest of the household. They had their own suite of rooms or their own wing, their own nanny or nurse, their own meals, their own activities. They wore children's clothes rather than copies of their parents' outfits, they read children's books and comics, they played in children's parks and playgrounds, they joined children's clubs and played children's games. They had new, expensive toys, their clothes were of the finest materials, they never

At family mealtimes, children were expected to behave with the impeccable manners that Nanny had taught them.

had to worry or concern themselves with money, and there was always someone – nanny, nurse or nurserymaid – to do everything for them.

On the other hand, despite the privileges of an aristocratic or upper-middle-class upbringing, wealthy boys and girls were generally not spoilt. They learnt strict rules of behaviour, were taught good table manners and instructed not to be rough or rude, they followed rigid routines in the nursery and learnt never to answer back, either to their nanny or their parents and other grown-ups. Despite a gentler approach, adults were still all-powerful, always right and always to be obeyed. Rosamond Lehmann wrote: 'No grown-up in my personal experience ever said sorry to a child in those days. None, in the event of inability to answer a question, ever confessed to simple ignorance.' Nanny, like the other adults, often refused to answer questions from inquisitive little minds and brought the conversation to an abrupt end with 'That's right, dear, be quiet now and eat up those lovely greens.' It was with nanny that the children spent most of their time. A new baby stayed with its mother for the first few months of its life, until it was weaned, and then it was given into the care of the nanny, who lived ate and slept with the children in the nursery, shut off from the rest of the house by a green baize door.

Life with Nanny

The top floor of the house was often given over entirely to the day nursery, the night nursery, the schoolroom, a small storeroom or kitchen, a bathroom and sometimes a separate room for Nanny. Otherwise she slept in the night nursery with the babies and younger children, and had no real privacy. Older children had their own room on a lower floor or next to the night nursery. In a large country mansion an entire wing had its own staircase, corridors, day nursery, night nursery, schoolroom, Nanny's room, a room for the nurserymaids, a kitchen and still room (or pantry) and bedrooms for the older children. Gervas Huxley writes: 'Our world was the nursery and servants' wing. All the first floor rooms opened out of a long corridor, glorious for races and games.' And Kenneth de Burgh Codrington, writing of his experiences while visiting wealthy friends in their country house, recalls the eldest daughter telling him that 'We have a wing of the house to ourselves . . . at least the schoolroom and the nursery are in the back wing. We don't usually go into the Great House unless Bart [her father] sends for us . . . we have a dining room to ourselves, of course. The babies are kept in the nursery.'

During the day Nanny organized nursery life with military skill, as Angela Brazil describes in her novel *The Fortunes of Philippa*: '. . . Nanny was a power in the household. She managed the nursery with the tactics of a general, reducing

Nannies usually wore black bonnets and black capes or coats for trips out of doors.

small rebels to a state of submission with admirable skill, and keeping order among her noisy little crew with a firm though just hand. She might not always be exactly pleasant but on the whole her moral atmosphere was like an east wind, bracing, though a little trying at times.'

Children saw little of their parents, and rarely took part in family events until they were considered old enough, at the age of fourteen or so, to sit with the adults at the dinner table. Their mother sometimes put her head around the nursery door during the morning to see that all was well, and sometimes a small child was allowed down to the dining-room to talk to Father while he ate his breakfast and to perhaps be fed little morsels of bread or roll spread with butter and marmalade as a special treat. But the day was spent with Nanny and the nurserymaids, and it was Nanny who dried tears, bathed and bandaged cut knees, listened to troubles and arbitrated in any squabbles. She washed, dressed, scolded, supervised and fed. She organized games and outings, she read stories, taught the alphabet and numbers, instructed in good manners, undressed and bathed, and then when evening prayers had been carefully recited, she popped her little charges into bed.

When the children reached the age of four or five, a governess or tutor was hired to teach them their basic lessons until they were sent off to public school or to a local day school, but it was Nanny who supervised life in the nursery, and the bond

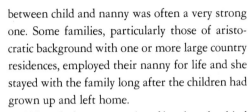

between child and nanny was often a very strong one. Some families, particularly those of aristocratic background with one or more large country residences, employed their nanny for life and she stayed with the family long after the children had grown up and left home.

Although there are stories of harsh and unkind nannies, most seem to have been much loved, and many children were heartbroken if their nanny left for any reason. The close bond with this surrogate mother figure did not mean that children did not also love their parents, but the relationship between parent and child was a very different one from what is normal today. Mother and Father did not have to worry about organizing the children's lives, or tidying up after them, or cooking for them and teaching them table manners. All the more mundane activities went on in the nursery, and when the family came together they were all dressed in their smartest clothes and absolutely on their best behaviour. When Mother dressed up for dinner parties or the theatre she had a magical quality, she always smelt of exotic perfumes and wore extravagant silks and satins. Father was always either setting off for his important work in a smart suit and bowler hat, or he too was dressed for the evening's entertainment. The children regarded them with awe and wonder and wished to please and be loved by such adored figures. In some houses there was a real closeness between parents and children. Sometimes it was the mother who taught the children

Books and music played an important role in Edwardian households.

to read and gave lessons in religion or French. Father often spent time in the evenings teaching them to play chess or draughts.

The Family House

The younger children hardly ever saw some of the rooms in other parts of the house. The lower ground floor or basement was usually occupied by the kitchens, sculleries, dairy, laundry and servants' rooms, and few children were allowed past the door, except at Christmas when they joined in the ritual mixing of the Christmas pudding. Cynthia Asquith recalls that 'The large-high-raftered realm with sanded floor, blazing fire, revolving spit and gleaming coppers, was the kingdom of a very great personage called the Cook who looked alarmingly like the Red Queen in *Alice in Wonderland*, but was nearly always gracious enough to allow us to beat up an egg, roll out dough or, best of all, toss a pancake.' The inside of the dining-room was rarely seen, except perhaps when children were allowed down to say good morning to their father before he disappeared to work, or for family prayers before breakfast, or for a magic lantern show on a Sunday afternoon. Diana Cooper admits: 'All fathers . . . had magic lanterns and slides of the Zoo and the Houses of Parliament and Niagara, but we thought ourselves unique and superior by having one – only one – of Father himself and my eldest sister Marjorie, taken in Scotland, with a background of moors.' The drawing-room was

visited every day when children of all ages were delivered into their mother's charge for an hour or so at about four or five o'clock. Here they were shown off to visitors, or asked to sing or recite poetry, or on quieter days they browsed through photograph albums or were read to, or were taken for a stroll in the garden with their mother, to look at the flowers. Parents' bedrooms and dressing-rooms were not places that children very often went except to say good morning to Mother while she lay propped against lace pillows, eating her breakfast or writing letters. Sonia Keppel tells how '. . . each morning I visited Mamma's room where, enchantedly, I played with all the lovely things she had worn the night before . . .. Then I migrated to Papa's room where, equally enchanted, I watched this benevolent giant eat a giant's meal. Two boiled eggs, two fried eggs, an omelette and kidneys and bacon usually made up his breakfast. I was allowed to crack the eggs with a knife, and to spread his buttered toast with jam. Alertly, I stood at his side with his arm round me, and it never occurred to either of us that I should sit down. Thereafter, I was allowed to watch him shave, and to watch him curl his moustache with tiny tongs.'

Since so little time was spent outside the nursery, memories are hazy. Cynthia Asquith recalls that 'Outside Nanny's special territory, the Nursery, I mistily remember how to my perceptions the remainder of the house gradually resolved itself into separate regions. The most enchanted of all was what the fat butler always called – the very name thrilled me – "Her Ladyship's Bood-War" – the special sphere of a lovely and loving being called "Mamma" . . . It was to this entrancing room that for that blissful part of the day called "After Tea" we rapturously repaired.'

The decor of the rooms below the nursery floor was generally lighter and airier than before. Although some people still favoured the draped mantels and dark furnishings of Victorian days, most rooms were decorated with paler colours, William Morris wallpapers and fabrics, and any wood panelling was much lighter than that of the previous century. Wicker chairs and sofas were favoured, as were large comfortable settees. Tables were draped with chenille, and gas or oil lamps were used in houses where there was still no electricity. Gone was the clutter of Victorian rooms, and the dark stuffy pretentious ornateness of those days. In its place was a sense of light and space, an air of well-being and ease and a more relaxed comfort. Style was discussed everywhere, new thought was given to the interior of the house. The 1908 Ideal Home Exhibition, launched by the *Daily Mail*, showed electric fires, steam washing machines, gas cookers, vacuum cleaners, shades for electric lights, telephones and furnishings that demonstrated the new simple lines of modern design. Even the garden received different treatment – there were flower-beds filled with colour instead of the dull shrubberies that the Victorians had loved so much; there was a croquet lawn, a tennis court, and tucked away in the corner a sandpit or an old tree with a rope swing. The light from the garden was encouraged into the house through windows that were no longer hidden behind velvet curtains but framed by bright linen and chintz drapes. Sunlight invaded the house and brought with it a sense of freedom.

In the Nursery

This new spirit continued up into the nurseries – corridors were lighter, wallpapers were brighter, electricity brought a flood of light into many homes at the magical touch of a switch. Although the furniture was often rejected from the more fashionable areas downstairs, it was arranged in rooms with colours on the walls, pretty wallpapers from such popular designers as Kate Greenaway, Randolph Caldecott and Walter Crane, and light streaming in through, whenever possible, south-

Kate Greenaway's characters appeared in books of nursery rhymes and games, alphabets, friezes and pictures.

After years of oil and gas lamps, electric lighting was a real household treat.

facing windows. Experts recommended that the nursery should be housed in a room that received plenty of light as children love sunshine. Ideal measurements for a day nursery were given in helpful manuals of the time as twenty-five feet long, twelve feet wide and approximately fifteen feet high. The windows were often barred for safety, but could be opened to let in fresh air. The floor was usually covered with a hard-wearing carpet, thick matting or practical, hygienic linoleum. Alternatively the floorboards were scrubbed and then painted a bright colour. Linoleum was

favoured by many as it was so easily cleaned after inevitable nursery accidents such as spillages of food, upturned paint pots or worse. In the middle of the room was a large sturdy table which served as the meal table, a place to spread books when homework was being done, an excellent base for jigsaws and board games, and a display area for scrapbooks, cigarette cards, cut-out dolls and painting books. The fireplace, with its coal or gas fire, was surrounded by pretty tiles decorated with favourite teddy bears or fairy-tale characters. A coal fire was thought the healthiest, since it helped

to create a draught that, with a window ajar, drew fresh air in. Around the fire was a high brass fender that protected the children from accidents and provided an ideal place for drying damp clothes and for warming the towels before bath-time.

Chairs in the nursery were practical and hard-wearing, and there was always a high chair for the baby. Mechanical high chairs were first introduced in the late nineteenth century and continued to be popular until well after 1914. The adjustable chairs were made of birch or beech and the wood was either stained or painted white. The top half of the chair stood on a sturdy base to provide a safe frame at the meal table, but this could be lifted off to make a low chair that sat on the floor but still held the child in place. A tray for food or toys slipped easily into position in front of the baby while strong leather straps gave extra security. Diana Cooper tells how, 'As I sat perched high in my baby's chair, strapped in with a tray for my food that, attached to the chair, came whirling over my head and imprisoned me safely, Nanny would feed me bread and milk. . . .' Adjustable high chairs could also be used as rockers and had bouncing seats and other novelty features such as bells and rattles that helped to amuse bored babies. Chairs were often made to fold away when not in use, allowing Nanny and the children maximum space for daytime activities. As children were gradually accepted into other family rooms, furniture makers started producing miniature versions of adult chairs, and the nursery often contained small bentwood, bow-backed, high-backed and cane-seated chairs that could also be used in the drawing-room or bedroom. Another very popular design was the cane-seated deport-ment chair that forced the child to sit bolt upright with a very straight back.

Around the nursery were shelves to hold books, favourite toys, dolls, teddy bears and tin toys. Corners of the room were the homes of animals on wheels that could be ridden in battles and adventures, a blackboard, a dolls' house and a well-used and much-loved rocking-horse. Other toys such as building bricks, jigsaws, packs of cards,

A comfortable pose for a portrait in a favourite chair.

board games and dominoes, were kept tidily in a big cupboard or chest, and Nanny was strict in ensuring that her charges always put things away when finished with.

Next to the day nursery, the night nursery was a cosy hideaway with beds for the baby, the smallest children and for Nanny. These had wooden or brass frames and horsehair mattresses. Brass beds had become fashionable in the nineteenth century in the days when the metal industries were developing cheaper methods of manufacturing. Earlier metal beds had been made of iron, but the new fashionable trend was for a basic iron frame with brass head and tail boards and trimmings. The resulting piece of furniture was lighter, easier to move and considered more hygienic. By the 1890s, porcelain or mother-of-pearl was used to add an elegant and decorative finish. On each of the beds were lace or linen pillows, linen or cotton sheets, warm woollen blankets and an eiderdown. A heavy quilt or embroidered bed cover was thrown over and a few colourful cushions added a finishing touch.

The flooring in this room was linoleum or wood, sometimes with a carpet, probably an old one that no longer had a place downstairs, on top. Against the walls was a wardrobe for the children's clothes (although this sometimes stood outside the door in the corridor), a pine or oak chest of drawers, a dressing-table with a free-standing mirror on the top, and a few chairs. Near the fireplace a large armchair had pride of place, for this was where Nanny sat sewing, mending or reading to the children. The gas or coal fire was surrounded by a high fender, just like that in the day nursery, and on it nightdresses and pyjamas

would be left to warm in the evening. More toys and books filled shelves and window-sills while baby's coral or ivory teething ring and pretty ivory rattle lay beside the cot or cradle ready to soothe and amuse in moments of distress. On the walls were religious pictures or moral verses decorated with floral borders. Cynthia Asquith remembers '. . . the all-pervasive smell of the then sovereign remedy, Pommadavine; but except for the one picture of the Infant Samuel saying his prayers and the enlarged photograph of my mother in court-dress and feathers, I can visualize curiously little of these rooms.'

Friends for the Children

In large wealthy households, children spent most of their time tucked away behind the green baize door, seeing only their nanny and nurserymaids, occasionally their parents, other servants around the house and garden, and other children who came to visit or to stay. Cook was likely to be very reluctant to allow meddlesome children past the door into her domain, so the kitchens were usually out of bounds. But other servants, although deferential to their employer's children, often had very friendly relationships with them and were prepared to joke and sometimes play with them. In Vita Sackville-West's *The Edwardians*, Sebastian and Viola, the children of the family '. . . had of course been on terms of familiarity with the servants, especially when their mother was away, and as a small boy Sebastian had counted among his treats a particular game that he played with Vigeon [the Steward]. Vigeon could not always be coaxed into playing it ... but he sometimes condescended, and taking Sebastian in his arms he would lift him up to a painting that hung in the pantry. Sebastian in his sailor suit would squeal and wriggle with excitement. The painting represented a still life of grapes and lemons beside a plate of oysters. Vigeon would make passes before the picture, finally making a gesture of picking a grape off the canvas, when lo! a real grape would appear between his fingers, and with a final, triumphant flourish he would pop it into Sebastian's mouth.' Gervas Huxley recalls that 'Most of the inhabitants of the maids' rooms were our close friends and allies.'

The gardener was often a friend for the children, although he would not tolerate feet trampling over his borders, or nimble fingers plucking strawberries and currants without his permission. But he would help out with seeds, bulbs and cuttings for little patches of garden that the children liked to cultivate and was always ready to offer advice and instructions to willing workers. And as long as they stayed in their bit of the grounds and did not disturb his plants and vegetables, he was a chum. This is how Cynthia Asquith describes the gardeners at her parents' home: 'Outside the house, hoeing and digging in the walled kitchen-garden, lighting bonfires, scything the lawns or rhythmically sweeping leaves off the paths, were four out-of-doors friends with gnarled weather-beaten faces, hands caked with earth and bodies bent and twisted like pollarded willows.'

Children who grew up on large country estates also had for company the families who lived in the estate cottages. Since the boys and girls from these families were of a lower class, it was not generally considered correct for them to be playmates, but they inevitably knew each other and in some cases were good friends. Freya Stark remembers a contrast in attitude: 'My mother kept us carefully away from anything that might contaminate – servants, nurserymaids or other children: but my father believed in barbarian foundation for the growth of human beings. . . .' Geoffrey Brady sums up the attitude of many people of the time: 'I could hear even at that age that they spoke badly and perhaps behaved roughly and things like that. But if they were good sorts and friendly, I don't think it mattered in the least.' Certainly Joan Poynder recalls no problem: 'I knew the village children. They used to come to tea with me. We visited a lot.' If children from different classes were allowed to mix, they rode ponies and bicycles together, climbed trees and adventured in the grounds of their large mansion or in nearby fields and countryside. But most children from well-to-do families would rarely have been allowed to go outside the house or the walls of the estate unchaperoned, and they spent their time with Nanny, other employees of the family, and their parents.

NANNY'S DOMAIN

Portrayals of typical Edwardian nannies in famous books and films still amuse and entertain modern audiences and readers. Mary Poppins was able to control children that previous nannies could do nothing with; she worked magic spells, she amused, disciplined, solved problems and acted as intermediary between her charges and troublesome adults; she knew about everything and was prepared for every possible eventuality. Nana, the large lumbering dog employed by Mr and Mrs Darling in J. M. Barrie's *Peter Pan*, treated the Darling offspring, Wendy, John and Michael, rather like puppies, carrying them off to bed on her back, nudging them into obedience with her nose and protecting them from harm. Although her position in the Darling household is totally eccentric and impossible, she somehow fits the perceived role of the cuddly, warm, gentle but firm guardian that was responsible for the early lives of so many children from middle- and upper-class families during the Edwardian era. Barrie wrote of Nana: 'She proved to be quite a treasure of a nurse. How thorough she was at bath-time; and up at any moment of the night if one of her charges made the slightest cry. . . . It was a lesson

Edwardian mothers left the practical care of young children to their nannies.

in propriety to see her escorting the children to school, walking sedately by their side when they were well behaved, and butting them back into line if they strayed.'

Book illustrations paint a picture of a trusted and loved person who created an atmosphere of security and warmth while at the same time teaching the children their table manners and how to mind their Ps and Qs, ordering each event with good, solid common sense. Of course there are stories of sinister and cruel nannies who tormented their charges with harsh words and unnecessary punishments, who undermined the authority of parents and treated the job as a rather tiresome chore that had to be born in order to earn a living wage. John Betjeman in *Summoned by Bells* describes how

Sarah, with orange wig and horsey teeth,
Was so bad-tempered that she scarcely spoke;
Maud was my hateful nurse who smelt of soap
And forced me to eat chewy bits of fish. . . .

But the majority of stories and memories are of women who were always there when the children needed them, who entertained, organized, scolded when necessary, cuddled, comforted and mothered. Katharine Chorley wrote of her nanny: '... as a human being she was like thin panned gold and I thought her very nearly perfect. I don't think I loved her so much as I loved my mother but I certainly felt more intimate and easy towards her. I was not quite nine when she left and I have never since suffered quite the same feeling of desolation that I did when I knew she was going.' C.S Lewis remembered his nanny as a blessing 'in whom even the exacting memory of childhood can discover no flaw – nothing but kindness, gaiety and good sense.'

So who were these wonderful nurses who played such a vital part in upper-class Edwardian households? They were in fact almost invariably working-class and had probably started their working lives at the age of thirteen or fourteen as nurserymaids, lady's-maids or housemaids. Most had no formal training in the care of children but relied on personal experience obtained at home with their own mothers and younger brothers and sisters. Among their scant possessions they would have had a good handbook that gave all the necessary information and instructions as to health care, discipline, behaviour and diet.

While in service as working nannies, they could continue to collect useful information and ideas from the new journals that started appearing in 1899. The first was *Nursing Notes* and this was followed in 1907 by *Baby – The Mother's Magazine* and *Creche News* in 1915. Though aimed primarily at mothers, these publications no doubt also helped the vast numbers of trained and untrained nannies who had to rely on their natural ability to cope with children and their energy and resourcefulness in order to fulfil the role of nurse, mother, teacher and friend.

Getting the Job

When a family decided that it needed a nanny, there were several ways in which a suitable candidate could be found. Firstly, there was the chance that one of the existing servants in the household may have the right qualities for the position. Secondly, the lady of the house could ask her friends and relatives if they knew of a suitable girl or woman. Very often, when the children of one family were old enough to go off to boarding school, their mother's sister or cousin was in need of a nanny, and so she stayed within the family, sometimes going back after a few years to the first

Situations for nannies and nurses were advertised in the Servants' Advertiser and Register.

young lady she had looked after in order to be nanny to her children. Thirdly, the family could advertise in a newspaper, journal or through an agency, and in this case would almost certainly have required a reference. But most families preferred to employ someone they knew or knew of through friends or family. No doubt, many mothers referred to the sensible advice of Isabella Beeton regarding the essential qualities of a children's nurse. In her *Book of Household Management*, published in 1861, she wrote: 'Patience and good temper are indispensible qualities; truthfulness, purity of manners, minute cleanliness, and docility and obedience, almost equally so. She ought also to be acquainted with the art of ironing and trimming little caps, and be handy with her needle . . . it is desirable that she be a person of observation, and possess some acquaintance with the diseases incident to childhood . . . .'

In a middle-class family a nanny usually stayed for about five years, by which time the children were occupied with governesses, tutors and school, and no longer really needed someone to wash and dress them. So Nanny moved on to a new position, sometimes keeping in touch by letter with her previous employers and children. In an aristocratic family, Nanny was usually employed for life, staying on in the nursery wing long after the children had left home. Nannies very rarely married, their first commitment being to the children, but very occasionally they would meet a suitable young man from among the

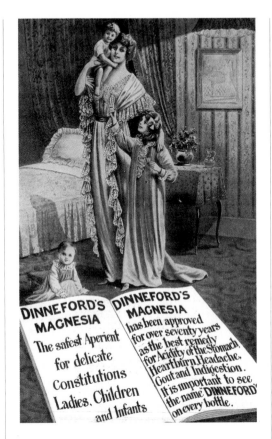

Nannies and mothers always kept a supply of standard remedies in the medicine cupboard.

household servants or from aqaintances outside the family, and they would leave their job in order to have children of their own. Widowed, older women sometimes went back to nannying, partly because they liked the company and enjoyed the job, but also because a position with a family ensured a good, steady salary and a secure home.

A Surrogate Mother

As soon as a baby was weaned it was handed into Nanny's care, and the child spent all its time in the night or day nursery. The mother's first duty was to her husband, but Nanny was always there for the children. Most nannies slept in the night nursery with the babies and younger children while older boys and girls had their own rooms where they were responsible for washing and dressing themselves. If the little ones needed attention during the night, it was Nanny who comforted them, saw to their needs and then settled them back to sleep. Parents slept untroubled through teething, minor ailments and bad dreams while Nanny capably sorted out any problems.

If Nanny had a room of her own, it was next to the night nursery. The room was sparsely decorated with cast-off furniture from downstairs, or with plain cheap functional pieces – a bed, a chair, a wardrobe, a chest of drawers, a washstand or basin and a sofa or armchair where she could relax.

Most nannies knew how to cope with all the eventualities of the nursery.

Nanny's Role

In some households, Nanny wore a black bodice and skirt and for trips outside she added a black coat and bonnet that tied under the chin with strong black velvet ribbons. In other houses she was dressed all in white with a spotless apron over the voluminous dress. She did not wear the stiff cap and cuffs that her nurserymaids were obliged to wear. Nanny's frock did not generally become grubby in the way that the maids' uniforms did, since she did not have to do any of the dirty chores. It was the maids that laid and lit the fire, blacked the hearth, cleaned the bedrooms, carried meals up from the kitchen and served the food, mopped up spills and tidied up after the children while Nanny oversaw their tasks and ensured that these were carried out quickly and efficiently. Diana Cooper explains 'I do not think that Nanny did the children's washing (the laundrymaid saw to that), and she had a nurserymaid to lay the table and dust and make our beds and dress my sister Letty and push the perambulator when in London.' Some wealthy families employed as many as four nurserymaids to keep the nursery running smoothly. In such a set-up, Nanny played a managerial ro!e and brought the children up while the maids scrubbed and cleaned, sorted dirty linen, emptied potties, stitched and mended and ran up and down stairs on missions to the kitchen. In some houses, the maids had to make anything up to a hundred trips a day up and down the stairs to fetch trays of food, jugs of hot water, piles of clean

linen, clean and dirty dishes, hods of coal and general household supplies. Diana Cooper remembers that '... the stairs were very exhausting, especially for the ever-changing seventeen-year-old nurserymaid who carried our trays up the last flight of four, and for the "boy" who carried them up the other three storeys. Many a time did we hear with joy the interminable clatter of a whole tray's fall, with its horrid mutton and cabbage and tapioca pudding.'

Nanny enjoyed the cleaner, pleasanter tasks. She washed and dressed the children, or chivied

Kensington Gardens was a perfect venue for afternoon outings with Nanny.

Edwardian perambulators
ranged from grand carriages to low
wicker-framed pushchairs.

them along while they dressed themselves, she did their hair, played with them, read to them, taught them their alphabet, organized games, took them for walks, supervised nursery meals and made sure that they were perfectly groomed, especially when they went downstairs to join their mother and father in the drawing-room. In more modest households, Nanny would have helped with at least some of the chores, but there was always a nurserymaid to bear the greatest burden of the grubbier, harder jobs. Occasionally the under-maids were allowed a short break from the chores and were left in charge of the children while Nanny made an occasional trip downstairs to have her supper in the servants' hall.

Nanny's Influence

Nanny's domain consisted of all the rooms and staff within the nursery floor or wing, and in this territory she was all-powerful. She made all the rules as to what the children could or could not do, say, eat and drink. Parents accepted, when they chose a nanny, that the nursery was her kingdom and that within it she had total control although some mothers found it difficult to hand over responsibility so completely to Nanny. Even in royal households, Nanny reigned supreme. She had more power and more involvement in the children's lives than tutors and governesses, who often thought themselves superior because of their education, and therefore came into conflict with down-to-earth Nanny. Often Cook and

Nanny would wage war over what the children were to be given to eat, who was to carry up the trays and who had the most influence in the household. Cooks were notorious for their rather imperious attitude towards staff, but Nanny usually gave as good as she got.

Although parents played a very important part in shaping their children's religious, social, moral and political attitudes, Nanny had an enormous influence purely and simply because she was with the children all the time. It was she who commented on behaviour, who instructed, informed and disciplined. Her sense of humour, her choice of literature and music, her sense of right and wrong inevitably rubbed off on the young people who spent all their time in her charge. On a social level, at least, mothers did not need to worry that their offspring were having their heads filled with working-class notions. Most nannies adhered to the attitudes of the families in which they worked. They taught the children that they were superior to the village children or the children of estate workers and that these others were much too rough to associate with nice children. Some identified so strongly with their employer's class that they became rather snobbish towards other servants and lower-class families. But most nannies accepted class divisions as a fact of life and worked within the system without prejudice. They took a very Christian attitude and taught the children that everyone was equal. Joan Poynder recalls that her nanny '. . . made me realize that

After nursery breakfast, children sometimes visited the grown-ups in the dining-room downstairs.

people were the same and you must not be a snob and you must not think of yourself better than anybody else. And that I never lost.'

Nanny's Concerns

Nanny had few worries about finances. Her position was secure – unless she did something frightful and was dismissed – and when one family ceased to need her she knew that, with a good reference or recommendation, she could easily find a new position. She had far less to be concerned about than her employers, since it was

when they cried, without the long-term burden of worrying what was to become of them or her relationship with them in five or ten years' time.

On a daily basis, however, Nanny took her position very seriously and made quite sure that the children knew right from wrong and learnt how to behave in all situations. Despite an increasing recognition of a need to behave more liberally towards children, Nanny based her disciplinary methods firmly on Victorian principles. These prescribed a rigid and strict attitude and were designed to prevent children from

they who had to earn the money to pay her, they who worried about their children's future, education and financial security. Nanny had only to worry about day-to-day tasks, and although she was very fond of the children, she knew that she did not have to bear ultimate responsibility for them. So she could enjoy their company, scold or praise them, laugh with them and dry their tears

becoming spoilt, even if they were brought up in a financially privileged situation. Everyday routines were categorically adhered to and involved restrictions and prohibitions in an effort to limit the amount of pleasure experienced by each individual. Cleanliness, washing, hair brushing and neatness of dress were insisted upon. There was to be no chattering at mealtimes and none in the night

Little girls were dressed in prettily frilled voile or muslin frocks.

nursery once the light was switched off. If a group of children was taken out by Nanny, they were expected to walk in a tidy, orderly crocodile, and if a child was naughty while out, he or she had to hold on to the pram or sit quietly beside Nanny on the park bench while the others played or made daisy chains. Children who persistently sucked their thumbs were made to wear gloves. On Sundays, some children were not allowed to play but were expected to read quietly so as not to disturb the peace of the 'Lord's Day'. If a child refused to finish food at one meal, the plate was kept in the pantry until the next meal, when it reappeared and was set in front of the obstinate child. If again it was left uneaten, again it was kept and again it reappeared, until it was eventually eaten. Children often had to face the same bowl of lumpy porridge or greasy gristle at each meal until he or she decided to be really brave and eat the wretched stuff. Diana Cooper remembers how her sister Letty could not swallow her food: 'Round and round it went in her mouth, colder and more congealed grew the mutton fat, further away receded the promising pudding, and very often I saw her unfinished platter put cold into the cupboard for tea. Nanny, typical of her date and dryness, trained us by punishment only, never by reasoning and persuasion.' And Cynthia Asquith writes: 'Oh! Those sickening glutinous lumps of sago, and the dread threat, "Now then, Cincie, if you don't eat your nice pudding up at once, you shall have it cold for breakfast." ' The only way to

move on to a more appetising meal was to eat the rejected food. Of course there were ways of making it disappear without actually eating it. A pet dog or cat under the table was extremely useful, but these were a rarity in the nursery, and so Nanny's attention had to be distracted or some reason found for getting her out of the room, whereupon the offending bacon or mutton fat was slipped down the back of the toy cupboard or chest of drawers, not to be discovered until the next bout of spring cleaning. Other restrictions were enforced as to what could be eaten, how much and when – bread and butter had to come before cake, and if you had jam on the bread and butter, then there was no cake. If cake was allowed, you only got one slice. Food was never to be left – not even grape pips and skins, brown bits in the bananas, burnt toast, dry crusts and lumps in the rice pudding. They all had to be eaten, and if they were left, well, you knew what would happen!

The one thing that all nannies were absolutely inflexible about was potty training. Washing dirty nappies in those days was not a very pleasant task and involved a lot of work for Nanny and the maids, so it was desirable to train babies to use the potty as early as possible – a dry clean baby pleased Nanny, and all children wanted to please Nanny. Training started in the first month or so of the baby's life, and as the children grew older, so they were expected to continue the morning routine. They were asked every day, even when they were much older, whether or not they had 'been'.

Nanny's strictness in this and in other nursery routines, meant that although the children adored her, they were also afraid of her unbending authority. This underlying fear often continued well into adulthood, and Nanny still ticked her children off, even when they were over twenty-one.

But all the restrictions and regulations were not meant unkindly. They were thought to be good for the child. They were designed to develop self-discipline, good manners, a clear understanding of right and wrong and a respect for others and for oneself. The prohibition of so many things meant that little things which we today would regard as perfectly ordinary, were then thought of as treats. An extra piece of cake at a special tea, jam on the rice pudding, a new ribbon for your hair, a new paintbox, a magazine with pictures to colour – little things like these gave enormous pleasure and created lighter moments in the very strict routine of everyday life in the nursery.

The nursery was kept spotlessly clean with a little help from modern disinfectants.

Carbolic and Cod Liver Oil

One of Nanny's most important roles was to look after the children's health. Somewhere in the nursery or in Nanny's room was the medicine chest and first aid box. The experts recommended that the emergency box should contain bandages, lint, cotton wool, pieces of old linen, adhesive plaster, safety pins, needles, thread, oiled silk or gutta percha (a rubber-like substance), tissue, scissors, forceps, carbonized olive oil, permanganate of potash crystals, a bottle for smelling salts and iodine for disinfecting cuts and grazes. The medicine chest, always kept well out of the reach of tiny hands, contained remedies for all the children's typical complaints such as colic,

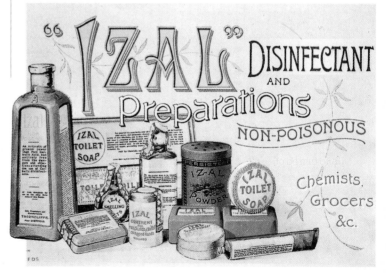

A trained nurse brought care and comfort to the sick room.

tummy aches, coughs and colds. It was extremely important to keep children healthy and strong to enable them to resist such diseases as tuberculosis, typhoid and diptheria, that were still common in the early years of the twentieth century. Surgery was still very dangerous, there was no national health service, dentistry was not yet a serious profession, and hospitals were considered to be places for the poor, while the rich were treated and nursed at home. Minor operations for tonsils and adenoids were carried out under the effects of ether or chloroform, and the patient was sometimes then cared for by a special nurse employed for the duration of the illness, or by one of the family servants. If a child did fall prey to a serious illness, a bed was often made up downstairs, or a special room was turned into a sick bay where the child could be carefully looked after. Sybil Pearce remembers how she and her mother suffered scarlet fever together: 'In those days it was not compulsory to go to a hospital for infectious illness. Nelly (the servant) hung a sheet soaked in Izal outside our bedroom doors and no-one was allowed to pass except herself. My father spoke to us through the bedroom window, standing in the garden.'

Although Nanny was obviously not equipped to cope with minor operations and serious illnesses, she was expected to know about all the less serious ailments and to have a remedy for them. An understanding of germs was well established by 1900 and Nanny battled constantly against microbes by having floors scrubbed with carbolic soap, rooms dusted and cleaned frequently, windows flung wide open to allow fresh air in and stale air out, rubbish bins emptied daily and flies kept under control. Her own and her maids' uniforms had to be spotless, hands were constantly washed, the children were bathed daily, and, most important of all, inner systems were perpetually cleaned out. Headaches and biliousness were blamed on a disfunction of the liver and bowels, and Nanny kept a large collection of emetics and laxatives in the medicine chest. Books dealing with the subject of the health of the household recommended that in all cases of illness 'the bowels should be kept well open' and Nanny knew that one of her main tasks was to insist that

the children develop regular habits. They were encouraged to drink as much water as possible, and olive oil, syrup of figs, senna leaves and pods,

epsom salts, fluid magnesia, cod liver oil, compound liquorice powder, brimstone and treacle and sulphur were all used to help keep the system regular. Tummy upsets were cured with cod liver oil or milk of magnesia, and bicarbonate of soda or slaked lime were given to prevent travel sickness or as a remedy for flatulence. Barley water was thought to aid digestion and was taken diluted in

Every nursery medicine chest contained a good stock of cough medicines.

milk or water. Colic was treated with a dose of sal volatile or dill water followed by a dose of castor-oil, which was a favourite medicine for all sorts of complaints. Mrs Beeton wrote of it: 'It is the safest of any to be found in the medicine chest for if it does no particular good, not perhaps being applicable to the case in hand, it has seldom been known to cause harm.' Formamint, a proprietary brand cure-all, claimed that it would ward off scarlet fever, sore throats and bad breath, while another favourite, Emerson's Bromo-Seltzer, was taken against headaches, neuralgia, nervousness, fatigue, constipation and upset tummies.

If a child was suffering from a cold, glycothymoline was put up its nose, and for coughs and colds, ammoniated tincture of quinine was administered. It had a hateful, bitter taste and children were reluctant to swallow it. A chest cold was treated by tying a muslin bag containing a hot linseed poultice round the child's neck so that the fumes would penetrate the nasal cavities, while another popular treatment involved a warm compress of camphorated oil on the chest. Earache was comforted with a hot water bottle or a large hot potato wrapped in a piece of flannel, and persistent headaches were dispelled by lying the patient down in a quiet, darkened room.

Of course, some nannies had no time for modern ideas and remedies and stuck to all the old Victorian favourites. J.M. Barrie satirized this attitude in *Peter Pan* and wrote of Nana: 'She had a genius for knowing when a cough is a thing to

have no patience with and when it needs a stocking round the throat. She believed to her last day in old-fashioned remedies like rhubarb leaf, and made sounds of contempt over all this new-fangled talk about germs, and so on.' But most children were dosed with at least some of the new patent medicines and treated according to new ideas. John Betjeman humorously sums up the Edwardian attitude to children's health in these lines from *Summoned by Bells*:

Come, Hygiene, goddess of the growing boy,
I here salute thee in Sanatogen;
Anaemic girls need Virol, but for me
Be Scott's Emulsion, rusks, and Mellin's Food,
Cod-liver oil and malt, and for my neck
Wright's Coal Tar Soap, Euthymol for my teeth.
Come friends of Hygiene, Electricity
And those young twins, Free Thought and Clean
    Air.

Although Nanny knew all about how to make the children better, her main concern was to keep them well, so that they did not suffer from all those tiresome complaints. She made sure that they got plenty of fresh air and sunshine and that they ate a healthy, balanced diet. She taught them to sit up straight at the meal table so that their spines grew correctly and their insides had a chance to function properly. She encouraged them to eat slowly and to chew each mouthful carefully, to eat up all the vegetables and porridge that

Ready prepared infant foods saved young mothers and maids hours of work.

provided roughage, and not to indulge in too many sugary foods. If a child was ill, she would ask Cook to send up beef tea, steamed white fish, minced chicken, scrambled or coddled eggs, barley custard pudding, blancmange or oatmeal gruel. The light, semi-liquid foods helped to build the child's strength and get him or her on to the road to recovery.

Nursery Philosophy

Nanny often had favourite sayings to encourage the children to do the things she wanted. To help horrid medicine down, she would say, 'Upsie daisy, hold your nose, swallow hard and down she goes!' Table manners and eating habits were the subject of many of her little quips. 'Eating toast crusts makes your hair curl, so eat them up', 'Save your breath to cool your porridge', 'If you don't eat up you'll never grow tall' and 'Wicked waste brings woeful want' were all standard sayings to urge the children to eat up. Good manners were encouraged with 'Sit up straight at the table so there's room for a mouse at the front and a cat at the back', 'No uncooked joints on the table' and 'You'll scrape the pattern off the plate'. At bedtime, Nanny assured the children that 'The sandman's on his way' and that they must go 'up the little wooden stairs to Bedfordshire' or 'up the wooden hill and down sheet lane'. A good long sleep was essential because 'The longer you sleep, the longer you'll grow', and if a child was out of sorts or grumpy at bedtime, Nanny vowed that 'All you

need is a night between the sheets to put you right.' These old sayings were a standard part of every nanny's repertoire, and she had one for all events and incidents. Children rarely got a straight answer to a straight question. Instead, one of Nanny's little sayings had to suffice. Alternatively they were told, 'Ask no questions and you'll be told no lies.'

Nanny's life was totally preoccupied with the children, and she rarely had any time to herself. She lived as part of the family, travelling with them whenever they went away or moved from their country house to their town residence. During her stay with a family, her life revolved around the needs of the children of that one family. If she had any free time during the day, while the children were at their lessons or resting, she would spend it making new clothes and sorting out laundry, bed linen, mending and darning. Dolls and their clothes often needed the attention of Nanny's careful needle, and toys or games needed sorting and tidying. Even in her own room, she was seldom left in peace for very long, since one of her brood would be sure to need attention to a minor cut or bump, or a ribbon put expertly back in place, or a shoe buttoned. It was only after all their needs had been seen to that Nanny could sit down and read a book, write a letter, have a snooze or make a cup of tea to help her relax after all the hours of constant caring, organizing, chivying, playing, encouraging and cuddling that filled each working day.

AN ORDINARY DAY

While the children of wealthy middle-class families were waking up in their cosy night nurseries under the watchful eye of Nanny, less privileged town children were being aroused from their sleep by the 'knocker-up'. At five o'clock every morning, an hour before work was due to start in the factories and mills, an elderly man walked the streets, carrying a long pole tipped with wires which he rattled against the windows. His clogs clattered in the empty streets and his voice echoed around the urban stillness as he shouted up to his customers. Workers were soon emerging sleepily from their modest terraced houses or cottages while children prepared for another day at school. Young boys raced off to do a paper round or help with the milk delivery before heading off to their lessons. Younger brothers and sisters scrambled into school uniform, or dressed in the one set of clothes that they possessed, ate their porridge or toast in a modest dining-room or humble kitchen, and then made their way in little straggling groups to the nearby elementary or secondary school.

In the night nurseries of wealthy households, the day began when the nurserymaid came in to clear out the ashes from the previous day's fire and lay and light a new one. The children might snuggle into Nanny's warm bed for a cuddle, or sit on top of the quilt and play with small toys. Then Nanny would get up and disappear behind a screen to wash or bath and dress in her neat uniform. Diana Cooper's nanny 'took her bath every morning behind the nursery screen on which Walter Crane's Sleeping Beauty, Yellow Dwarf, Beauty and the Beast, etc. were pasted. I was given a Marie biscuit to allay my curiosity and never did I peer through the screen chinks.' Nanny's first job was to get the small children and babies out of bed ready for their morning wash or bath. Older children used the bathroom in the main house or the nursery bathroom, or else they washed at the washstand or basin in their own rooms. The little ones were bathed in a large enamel tub in front of the fire in the nursery. Towels and clothes were warmed on the fender that protected the children from the blazing gas or coals. The little bodies were scrubbed and rubbed and swathed in thick towels. Babies were washed with castile soap and water softened with a little bicarbonate of soda or borax. It was an accepted

After breakfast it was time for lessons at school or in the nursery.

principle that a normal, strong, healthy baby should be bathed every day and twice in hot weather. Older children were expected to bath as often as possible, preferably daily.

Dressed and Ready

After the bathing or washing, it was time to dress. Babies were wrapped in a binder, a napkin or nappie, a flannel petticoat, a gown, a woollen jacket, a bib and booties. The quality and elaborateness of these various garments, and the amount of lace, frills and ribbons that decorated cuffs, collars, hems and bonnets depended on the wealth of the family.

Children of all ages wore masses of underclothes – vests, combinations, bodices, petticoats, etc. Young girls were often required to wear long woolly combinations, knitted cummerbunds, a pair of stays, cotton drawers, woollen bloomers, flannel petticoats, over all this a cotton petticoat and finally a frock. Boys wore less. Very young boys from upper-class families were dressed identically to girls in frilly gowns, and their hair was left to curl gently down around the face. As they grew older they were put into white drill (stout cotton cloth) or sturdy woollen sailor suits which were worn with black, white, navy or brown stockings or socks. For Sundays and special occasions, they often wore velvet suits with knee breeches, lace collar and cuffs and, for church or visiting, a 'po' hat – a soft, grey, hat shaped rather like a chamber pot. Rougher, poorer children

considered the sailor suit to be rather 'cissy' and opted for wide trousers that came down over the knee, stockings, a jacket and a bonnet with a button on the top.

Fashions for boys were strongly influenced by the appearance in 1908, in one of the Sunday newspapers, of Buster Brown, a comic strip character who always wore knee length bloomers, a double-breasted, belted jacket, a white collar, a black bow and a straw boater. Older boys were therefore very fashionable in the very popular Norfolk jackets, (worn over a singlet, woollen vest or shirt) knee breeches or plus fours, an Eton collar and a cap or boater. Kenneth de Burgh Codrington writes of his stay at the house of rich friends: 'On Sunday, Emily put out my best clothes for me, with an Eton collar, a black tie, and a clean handkerchief. I knew that Lowseley and Stephen [his friends] would be wearing the same sort of clothes as I was, for throughout the middle and upper classes at any rate children's clothes varied in quality and not in cut, in quality and in details.' For special occasions boys sometimes wore rather drab suits that echoed their father's attire, and they were expected to complete the outfit with a bowler hat that tended to be uncomfortably tight.

Little girls were dressed in white or cream frilly muslin or voile dresses with deep bands of embroidery on the yoke and the hem. The frocks had high waists, large collars and wide sleeves that were gathered at the shoulder and remained full all the way down to the cuff. In winter, velvet was

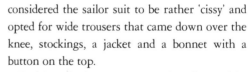

popular for dresses of the same style or for pinafores that were worn over silk or voile blouses. Smocks were also considered very smart for little girls and were made of white washing silk and smocked with silk threads at the yoke and the

Winter fashions for boys offered by Peter Robinsons of Oxford Street.

cuff. Socks and stockings were white or black and were worn with shoes indoors and with tight buttoned boots out of doors.

Older girls wore larger versions of their little sisters' garments. Especially favoured were yoked frocks, worn with wide sashes at the waist and elaborate details on collars and tight-fitting cuffs. Kenneth de Burgh Codrington writes: 'It was a hot, still day and Eleanor was wearing another of her white broderie anglaise frocks, full in the skirt and wide at the shoulders, tied with a blue sash. On a chair by her lay her large floppy leghorn straw hat, also tied with a blue ribbon. There were a great many other girls of thirteen dressed exactly like that in England on that clear August Sunday.'

The pinafore was also extremely popular, and evolved into the gym-tunics which were worn at school for games lessons, and, by 1910, as standard school uniform. By 1914, girls' dresses had a dropped waist – somewhere above the thighs – with a few inches of frill or kilted skirt below the belt. This was not a very comfortable or practical style, as it did not allow the child much freedom of movement and it split easily under the strain of exuberant activity. Older girls also wore the full skirts and neat waisted jackets that had developed as a result of the new craze for cycling. Knicker-bockers and shorter skirts were now very popular and extremely practical.

All children, of all ages, wore hats in winter and summer. In winter, a fur bonnet and a warm, woollen coat with fur trimmings kept out the cold, while hands were plunged into fur muffs or woollen mittens. The only part of the body that was exposed in cold weather was the face which could just be seen amid folds of warm fabrics and huge satin bows that held bonnets in place.

Curling Tongs and Pudding Basins

Once Nanny or the nurserymaid had overseen the ritual of getting dressed, hair had to be brushed and tidied. Babies' hair was allowed to grow until the age of two or four years old, when boys had their first haircut and were put into trousers. For family haircuts, wealthy people usually employed a professional, and a visit to the barber might yield a brightly coloured balloon as a reward for a well-behaved child. Usually, Nanny or nursemaid washed the children's hair, and in houses with no running hot water, this was quite a complicated operation, as Rachel Ferguson describes: 'Every so often one had a shampoo in conditions almost impossible to the shampooer. For it involved heating kettles in the nursery, filling cans, and then functioning in a basin on the nursery table. The shampoo was yellow and called egg julep and was quite delicious – it smelt of lemon curd and came out of round white china boxes.' Nannies, maids and poorer families cut and managed their own hair. Boys' hair was worn short and neat, brushed across the head from a tidy side parting. For an amateur cut an upturned pudding basin was set firmly on a boy's head to ensure a trim finish,

While Nanny saw to the babies, older children washed themselves.

while little girls grew their hair and had to endure curling tongs, curling rags, papers and clips to tease it into ringlets and waves. Girls' locks were parted in the middle and plaited, or the front sections were taken back and tied in a large bow on the top of the head. Hair ribbons of all descriptions were an important part of hair dressing and pocket money was often spent on new ones and on the large black taffeta bows that adorned the top of the head or the nape of the neck.

The Day Begins

When all the children were washed and dressed, and had brushed, tidy hair and clean teeth, it was time either for breakfast or for morning prayers. In modest middle-class households, breakfast was a family meal taken in the dining-room, and unless the family were particularly religious, the only prayer to be said before eating was 'Grace'. In upper-class families, the older children were sometimes fed before joining the rest of the family and the staff for prayers in the dining-room, while Nanny said prayers in the nursery with the babies. Gervas Huxley tells how 'The prayers were always read by Grandfather. Back to the nursery we children then went for breakfast, while the grown-ups got down to an enormous meal laid out in plated dishes on the sideboard.' One thing Rachel Ferguson could never work out: '. . . how did the current cook manage to attend prayers while preparing breakfast for up to eight people?' The

children's breakfast was sent up to the day nursery from the kitchens and usually consisted of porridge, boiled eggs, scrambled eggs or bacon and eggs, followed by toast and marmalade or jam. During breakfast, Father might pop in to say good morning and plant a kiss on golden curls before going off to work in the chauffeur-driven family car, or by public transport.

Time for Lessons

After prayers and breakfast came lessons. While working-class children scampered off to the village or neighbourhood school, and some lower-middle-class children set off for a private day school, most middle- and upper-class children over the age of five were taught at home by a governess or tutor. He or she arrived daily, or in large households lived in, and taught the children their basic lessons in English, mathematics, history, geography and sometimes French. At the age of seven, boys were often sent off to 'prep' school, where they boarded during term time, or to a nearby private day school. Girls usually continued their studies with their governess until they too were sent to a day school or a boarding school and then on to a finishing school. If Nanny did not have any younger children to cope with, it was often she who accompanied the children to school in the morning and met them in the afternoon. Otherwise, the family chauffeur or coachman drove them in the car or carriage, or a nurserymaid walked with them to make sure that they arrived safely. Under fives spent the morning with Nanny, learning the alphabet and how to count and say tables. Diana Cooper wrote in her autobiography: 'Nanny taught me my letters on building-blocks and taught me to read without tears by the ripe age of four. I learnt that E was like a little carriage with a little seat for the driver, that G looked like a monkey eating a cake, and later that the pig was in the gig and how ten men met in a den ... Nanny sat and I stood by her side, reading aloud, as I followed her guiding pencil, from *Little Arthur's England*.'

The life of the children old enough to work in the schoolroom with a governess was often quite separate from that of the youngest infants, as Diana Cooper recalled: 'Sometimes the nursery would visit the schoolroom and be impressed by its age and intelligence, its aviary of canaries and bullfinches, and its many pugs, the only breed of dog considered "safe with children".... The schoolroom visited the nursery only when they were dressed as musketeers or Romans or clowns and were desperate for an audience. The nursery did not have pets. It had Nanny, who was all and everything.'

High Days and Holidays

During holidays from school lessons, children from all different backgrounds amused themselves with toys and games, and outdoor activities and adventures. Working-class children were wrapped up against the cold in winter, given a sun hat in summer and sent out into the streets or nearby fields to find their own entertainments, while mothers scrubbed and dusted, washed and ironed, shopped and cooked. Older boys and girls took responsibility for younger brothers and sisters, keeping them occupied and out of mischief, and pushing the baby's pram around with them, so that they all got plenty of fresh air, and mother was left in peace to do all the necessary chores. Flora Thompson describes what happened in Lark Rise: 'Around the hamlet cottages played many little children. . . . Every morning they were bundled into a piece of old shawl, crossed on the chest and tied in a hard knot at the back, a slice of food was thrust into their hands and they were told to "go play". . . .' They played in the streets with marbles and stones, skipping ropes and hoops until it was time to go back home for dinner or tea. In winter the only way to keep warm was to

run around, and hands were kept from freezing with old tins stuffed with scraps of rag that were set alight. Rural children had the freedom of the countryside and played in farm fields and woodland, fishing in ponds, riding ponies, picking wild flowers and creating their own excitement.

Children who grew up on large estates or in houses with big gardens played happily in parkland and shrubberies, riding bicycles, climbing trees, chatting with gardeners and game keepers and looking after their own patch of garden. Freya Stark loved being outside: 'The garden gave that delight of something going on all the time, which the world gives later to happy people. It WAS the world, with vagueness of chaos and the unknown beyond the wooden palisades.' Henry Vigne speaks of his parents' old-fashioned shrubbery which was 'all laurels and things and it was a lovely sort of place, you could dive into it. And the first thing you did when you left the house was to hare off and dive under the bushes and go and sit in there and discuss what you were going to do, because you were safe from grown-up interference. We had a four-acre meadow and an orchard and the house and garden.' Kenneth de Burgh Codrington tells how house rules were explained to him by his wealthy friends: 'You see, the rules really mean that we're expected not to make a nuisance of ourselves. Otherwise we do what we like, at any rate in the holidays. It's really common sense. For instance, getting wet and muddy and making a mess is against the rules. It

Country children amused themselves happily in fields and lanes until it was time to go home for dinner.

gives trouble, you see?' But, Kenneth noted that Eleanor, the thirteen-year-old daughter, 'was quite willing to tuck her frock into her bloomers and wade in the stream with us or clamber about in the woods. Girls wore a great many clothes, though they were simple enough and nothing to spoil.'

Wealthy parents who owned large estates allowed their children a great deal of freedom to play and adventure in the estate grounds, and sometimes beyond the perimeter fence since there was little in those days that could be of danger to a group of sensible children. But parents and Nanny liked to know where they were going. Kenneth's friends explain the system: '... we write it on a slate in the lobby downstairs, I mean, if we're going far, out of the grounds, for instance. And we have to be punctual for meals, so as not to upset the servants. And we're not allowed to saddle a horse without permission. And we're not allowed to take fruit from the walls or hot-houses.' Given these various restrictions, children were free to roam and play wherever they pleased. But a strict framework of discipline surrounded the lives of most youngsters, and they were expected to respect routines and adhere to a code of manners and behaviour that was taught through-out their childhood by parents, governesses, schoolteachers and nannies.

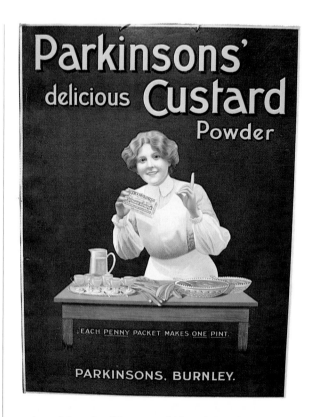

Stew and Roly Poly Pudding

Mealtimes were Nanny's opportunity to drum good manners into the children and at the table she would be continually training them in social etiquette, teaching them to think of others before themselves, to make sure that guests were comfortable and happy, to avoid discussing subjects that would shock adults and visitors. So when lunch arrived from the kitchens after a morning of hard work or tiring play, Nanny would launch into her usual instructions and comments. Lunch was the main meal of the day and consisted of meat and two vegetables and a pudding or pie with custard. Rice pudding with jam, spotted dog, baked jam roly poly, apple crumble and steamed sponges were all standard favourites. Rachel Ferguson remembers '... liquid chocolate and sponge fingers and "mock eggs" composed of squares of

Pudding was not complete without a generous serving of custard.

sponge cake, each with a thick ring of whipping cream enclosing a halved peach or apricot. Baskets concocted of hollowed-out castle puddings filled with cream, jam and chopped cherries, with a handle of angelica, and "fluffy pudding" which had a basis of delicious yellow stodge covered with stick-jaw meringue.' In more progressive upper-class homes and in more modest middle-class households, the older children and sometimes those as little as five or six years old ate lunch in the dining-room with their mother or with both parents, if Father came home to lunch. To do this they had to be able to manage their own knife and fork correctly and without making any mess, since Nanny was not there to help. Sometimes, Mother entertained guests to lunch and the children were taken down to be shown off but not to eat. Diana Cooper recalls: 'My mother entertained occasion-ally at two o'clock luncheon. Very beautiful women were always round the table ... I would come down in my embroidered-with-wheat lawn frock and scarlet shoes and stand by my mother's chair while she plucked admiringly at my hair and let it flutter slowly through her fingers. No one saw me with her eyes.'

A Walk in the Park

For children who did not spend the day at shool, the early part of the afternoon was set aside for a short rest, when they would sleep or be read to by Nanny. Then it was time for fresh air and exercise. Sometimes Nanny organized special outings to

the shops or the zoo, but the regular event was a walk to a nearby park. In Esther Stokes' nursery, 'We had a big fire of course and a high fire guard and it was the days of button hooks and Aggie'd say "Come along children, now we're going out for a walk," and we'd all rush to the fireguard and get our favourite button hooks to button our boots up with.' It was an accepted practice to take babies out as often as possible after the age of one month, and

At the Round Pond in Kensington Gardens there were ducks to feed and boats to sail.

as long as the weather was fine and warm. Other children were wrapped up in coats, gloves and hats to suit the season, and off they went, baby nestling amongst billowing layers of sheets and coverlets, capes, bonnets and shawls while the older brothers and sisters walked beside or behind Nanny in a very tidy little group. Gervas Huxley remembers these outings: 'The daily routine of children in our part of London included morning and afternoon walks in Kensington Gardens. Inside the Gardens, the Round Pond was our favourite. Here I sailed my boat and watched the other boats of all shapes and sizes. Other times we would trundle our hoops along the Broad Walk or round the shores of the Serpentine.' Hyde Park and Kensington Gardens were the great meeting places for nannies. Some would walk their prams for miles in order to meet up with other nannies. The paths in the parks thronged with prams and small children. As the prams were wheeled along, fine ladies and gentlemen in carriages and on horseback would sometimes stop to enquire whose children they were. When the nannies stopped and parked the prams safely, babies were lifted out and allowed to stretch their limbs and fill their lungs with fresh air, while toddlers were allowed to run around, pick daisies, feed the ducks, watch the squirrels and rabbits, or

Nanny occasionally managed to meet a suitor while out walking with the children.

play with their hoops or spinning tops while nannies gossiped and knitted together on the park benches. In Hyde Park, there was a balloon woman who sold brightly coloured balloons and windmills on sticks. Well-behaved children might be permitted to spend a little of their pocket money on one of these colourful toys, but woe betide a naughty girl or boy, for their freedom was curtailed and the miscreant had to stand or sit by Nanny and rock the pram.

Nanny organized other outings in order to get her charges out into the fresh air as often as possible, in summer and winter. There were drives in the donkey cart, or trips by horsedrawn bus or tram to the zoo or to the shops to buy ribbons or fabrics. But the little group never went very far, for they had to be back in time for nursery tea. This was a cosy, comfortable meal, and many look back on the nursery tea with great affection. Nanny was less severe than at other meals, and dolls, teddy bears and golliwogs were often included in the feast. In winter, muffins, crumpets and bread were toasted on the open fire, and in summer, banana sandwiches or sardines on toast made a deliciously appetising meal. Bread and butter was followed by sponge cakes, gingerbread and biscuits, while tea or milk was drunk from mugs and cups decorated with favourite fairy-tale characters and pictures from nursery rhymes.

Occasionally, children accompanied their mother when she went 'calling'. Cynthia Asquith says: 'This was not always an enjoyable treat, for

my fate, whether or not I was welcome, was to be precipitated into the nursery or the schoolroom of the children of the house and left to their mercies while our respective mothers conversed.' When Mothers entertained friends and neighbours to 'At Home Teas', children were sometimes asked to help look after the guests. Sybil Pearce '... was allowed to "hand round" the silver cake basket to the accompaniment of soft laughter, rustling skirts and the intermittent ringing of the front doorbell. I was quite pleased to do this as I knew that in the kitchen, waiting for me, was an exact replica of the little sponge cakes coated in soft chocolate whirls ....' And Geoffrey Brady remembers '... all these people being grandly shown in and putting cards on a silver tray in the

It was a thrill to be allowed to offer cakes to Mother's elegant visitors.

hall . . . and being ushered into the drawing-room. Occasionally I was allowed in for a few minutes.'

Some lucky children even entertained the King to tea. Sonia Keppel was one of them. 'Sometimes, King Edward (Kingy) came to tea with Mamma and was there when I appeared at six o'clock. On such occasions he and I devised a fascinating game. With fine disregard for the good condition of his trousers, he would lend me his leg, on which I used to start two bits of bread and butter (butter side down), side by side. Then bets of a penny each were made (my bet provided by Mamma) and the winning piece of bread and butter depended, of course, on which was the more buttery. . . . Although the owner of the Derby winner, Kingy's enthusiasm seemed delightfully unaffected by the quality of his bets.'

An Hour of Enchantment

After tea it was time for the magic hour when children visited their mother or parents in the drawing-room. First they were washed and changed into smart clothes, then they had their hair tidied, and were generally made ready to go down into the adult part of the house. Freya Stark says of these visits: 'There was a change in the atmosphere, a sort of temple feeling, when we passed through the green baize door. . . .' into Mother's realm. For Gervas Huxley, 'After nursery tea it was the invariable routine that we were changed into best clothes and escorted down to the drawing-room for an hour or so with Mother until bath and bed-time. The hour was usually spent in being read aloud to by Mother, while I lay on the floor and scribbled drawings on half-sheets of note paper. Mother had a great gift for reading aloud. Walter Scott's novels were our favourites. I suspect that Mother must skilfully have skipped dull passages, as we were never bored.' Esther Stokes says of her mother: '. . . my vivid recollection is that she would sit on a very big sofa and we'd sit all around her and took turns sitting beside her so that the one who was alongside her could see the book, and she read to us.' Cynthia Asquith's mother '. . . would read us fairy stories, or what I loved even more, Scotch ballads . . . . In this cherishing room there was a whispering snapping wood-fire . . . a Lear's Non-sense Book, in which we were allowed to colour pictures, and a large cupboard full of special toys.'

After a tiring day, Nanny led her charges up the stairs to the night nursery.

The time was sometimes spent looking at family photograph albums, listening to music on the gramophone, walking in the garden, reading poetry, playing the piano and singing together, or talking politely to visitors. If Father was at home he often spent time with the children, teaching them to play chess or cribbage, or reading adventure stories to them in his study. But the hour passed all too quickly, and Henry Green '. . . used to come down alone from five to six and each time I hoped they would not hear the clock strike bed time' – for then the children were separated from parents again and led back upstairs to Nanny's domain, to baths, prayers and bed. Older children were allowed time to play with trains, cars, dolls and other toys before they too were tucked up for the night. Children who had spent the day at school might have homework to complete before the next day's lessons, and Madge Hodson tells how she used to do hers lying on her tummy on her bedroom floor. Before she settled down to work she paid a visit to cook in the kitchen and chose something for her supper, which she ate upstairs while she worked.

Tiny tots were bathed or washed in front of the nursery fire. Sonia Keppel describes the fun she had while staying with friends: 'The culminating amusement of each day was in the nursery-bath, which had a lid on it, casually laid back against the wall. As this provided the risk of total eclipse, it gave our ablutions a particular thrill. The bath itself was filled with toy battleships and boats and floating animals. . . . Like sea-monsters we sat, swamping flotillas of sailing ships and dreadnoughts, until the last drop of water gurgled through the plug-hole and beached the lot.' And Cynthia Asquith recalled: 'Then there was the evening bath – the house boasted of only one bath-room and for baby legs this was a good five minutes walk from the nursery – a low circular tin affair, placed on a flannel spread out before the fire. I can see the brown hot-water can; feel the comfort of the enfolding bath towel warmed on the high fender around which there seemed always to linger a delicious small of hot-buttered toast.'

Bedtime

After the bath, little arms and legs slid into warm pyjamas, and then it was time for prayers. Herbert Read remembers the ritual in a modest middle-class home: '. . . in the sitting-room where we spent most of our life a lamp was lit, with a round glass shade like a full yellow moon. There we were bathed before the fire, said our prayers kneeling on the hearthrug and then disappeared up the steep stairs lighted by a candle to bed.' Prayers were part of the bedtime routine, and most children used the same simple verses or lines asking 'Please God, bless Papa and Mamma', or recited the Lord's Prayer. Nanny or Mother stood listening while little heads were bowed over folded hands as the children kneeled beside their beds.

Once they were tucked up, Nanny often fed them a hot drink of cocoa or a light snack. Cynthia Asquith wrote: 'Then the warm sweetness of "breadandmilk" . . . was enjoyed after we had been tucked up in the two little cots that, divided by Nannie's bed, were close enough for whispered conversations carried on long after we had been consigned to sleep. . . .'

While the children were preparing for bed, their parents would be dressing for dinner or getting ready to go out to theatres, concerts or other people's dinner parties. Dinners at home could mean entertainment for the younger members of the family. For Katharine Chorley, 'Dinner parties were fun . . . because I could lie on the floor of the gallery and peer through the balusters at the guests going into the dining room and then scuttle down to the back premises in the hope of snaffling a mouthful of succulent food as the dishes came out from the table.' Before guests arrived, parents would usually spend a little time in the night nursery reading or telling stories

Before being tucked up for the night, dolls had to say their prayers too.

FAMILY PRAYERS.

before kissing the children good night. Freya Stark's mother 'would come to kiss us in our beds or tell a story before she went down to her guests, and we waited for her as if she were an angel, with her white shoulders and necklace of amber, and gown of grey satin covered with pink flowers, decorated with black velvet bows.'

Then, when the story was finished, it was time for the lights to be turned out or the candles extinguished, no more chattering and off to sleep.

Weekend Activities

Saturdays were much the same as weekdays except that there were no lessons. Instead, the morning was spent playing or working at some hobby – sketching, making scrapbooks, reading – and then the afternoon outing was for spending pocket money in the toyshop, sweet shop or at a fairground or market.

Sunday was a sacred day on which, in many households, sports, games and toys were not allowed. The family went to church once or twice every Sunday, dressed in their best clothes. Children either sat through the service with their parents, or were taken to Sunday School; some were expected to attend both. At Sunday School, the children learnt to chant the names of the books of the Bible and were taught stories from the Old and New Testaments. They coloured pictures and stuck religious images on to special cards and books. Some loved it and looked forward to their visits. Others were bored and did not think that they learnt anything useful.

Of course, not everyone went to church, and fathers often took their offspring out for a walk in order to work up an appetite for Sunday lunch. Madge Hodson's father was one of these, but did not seem to understand that little legs grew tired rather sooner than adult ones, and would march his sons and daughters quite a distance before realizing that they were flagging. It was hard to decide between church with Mother or an exhausting walk with Father.

During the afternoon hour with their mother, children often strolled in the garden, learning the names of the flowers.

*On Sundays,
everyone walked to
church dressed in
their best clothes.*

In towns, the streets were full of people parading in their best clothes, chatting with aquaintances and friends, gentlemen raising their hats to passing ladies and children trying to amuse themselves while parents gossiped and passed the time of day before going home for lunch. Sunday lunch was a special meal, when all the family would be at home. There were often visitors and in more modest homes adults and children ate together in the dining-room. In upper-class houses, visiting children and their nannies joined the group in the nursery for a roast with all the trimmings. Rachel Ferguson's Sunday luncheon 'featured large sirloins of Scotch beef and I can smell and taste it still ... with the sirloin went square slabs of the kind of Yorkshire pudding that only cooks in private service seem able to make. ... The family carved for, the joint was sent into the kitchen, and if anybody wanted second helpings it had to be rung for.'

The afternoon was for walking, visiting and enjoying time together. Some routine activities were more a duty than a pleasure, however. Diana Cooper recalled how, every Sunday, her family and all the staff 'made a tour of the demesne. Soon after lunch, church clothes were changed for equally long, close-fitting costumes. The pony chaise was ordered for my grandfather and a groom to lead it.' The party toured the stables, the gardens, the poultry yard, the dairy and the kennels. 'It was an exhausting walk and my legs were short. I got a lift sometimes in my grandfather's lap in his chaise, but it was hard on the polite and reluctant men and women who trudged a good three miles, the ladies gathering up their long skirts in their little frozen hands.' But other families enjoyed visits from grandparents, aunts and uncles, and the afternoon and evening were spent singing hymns and popular songs around the piano, or family members performed party pieces, doing magic tricks, reciting poems, playing musical instruments and singing. The evening passed happily, and it was with reluctance that the children trudged up the stairs to bed, wishing that tomorrow could be Sunday too, instead of an ordinary Monday of lessons and weekday routines.

What hours of fun could be had driving round the family estate in a model car.

IN THE SCHOOLROOM

Before 1870, children in England were educated according to their parents' ability to pay the fees of private schools, and to the existence and availability of free, voluntary schools run by charities and religious bodies. After 1870, 'Board Schools', financed from local education rates, were established in urban areas, and particularly where there were few church schools. Most of these schools concentrated on the teaching of reading, writing and arithmetic, but their achievements were not remarkable. Neville Cardus '... attended what was known as a Board School, a place of darkness and inhumanity. I learned scarcely anything there, except to read and write. For four years only did I attend school, delicate years and miserable....' Florence Atherton was luckier at her school. 'It was a Catholic school. All of us went to the same school.... The eldest looked after the young ones. The boys and girls were separate, the boys upstairs and the girls down. But it wasn't a school that punished people a lot....'

In these early days, infants often sat in a circle on the floor, grouped around the teacher, as she pointed with her long stick to the letters on the blackboard. Then they traced the shapes for themselves in 'little trays filled with sand. We made our letters and figures with a stick like a pencil.... Later we had a slate and a slate pencil which made a horrible noise as the whole class worked.' Older children sat on hard wooden benches behind their desks and silently did their copy writing and sums.

By 1901 the best of the Board Schools had already started to organize secondary education, but politicians and academics realized that the entire system of primary and secondary teaching was inadequate. Buildings were too small, often unhealthy and badly equipped, classrooms were overcrowded with between forty and sixty children in one class, many of the pupils were cold and hungry throughout the day, and most teachers, some of whom were under sixteen years of age, had had no formal training, although many were thorough, hard-working and extremely dedicated. One young teacher, writing in 1901, '... had to teach every subject as if our lives depended on it.... My first Head Mistress was a martinet who was determined that her young staff should work.... Each teacher was wholly responsible for

Hard work at school was encouraged and rewarded with yearly prizes.

her class and had to teach every single subject, even music, be she ever so unmusical.'

Many children played truant, partly because for them the schoolroom held no charm, lessons made little sense, teachers were often frightening, and punishments were severe, and partly and more importantly because parents needed what

The School Board Officer stopped any children he came across in the street to ask why they were not at school.

little money their children could earn from full- or part-time jobs. The school attendance officer, known as The School Board Man, who would arrive from time to time in a uniform, a peaked cap and a very fierce expression, was much feared and was commonly regarded as a sort of police-man. Front doors slammed as truanting pupils

escaped to a safe hiding place, while in the classroom teachers and pupils alike were intimi-dated by his and the school-inspector's unbending harshness and cold attitude. A.L. Rowse clearly remembers 'Episodes like the inspector calling in Standard 11 and asking what change you would have from £1 if you had spent so much and so much adding up to 14s 6½d – or some awkward figure like that.'

Uninspired Teaching

Teaching was dull and very formal, teachers believing that they merely had to cram as many facts into the young heads as possible. The more facts a child could remember, the more intelligent he or she was believed to be. In some classrooms, badly trained teachers did not even try to occupy the rows of students sitting facing them. Often the children sat doing nothing or were required to read silently while Sir or Miss marked books and registers or even sat reading the daily newspaper. A Board School of 1900 was supposed to cover a curriculum that included arithmetic, reading, writ-ing, algebra, chemistry, scripture, grammar, geo-graphy, history, botany, singing, drawing, geometry, science and drill. This seems a comprehensive and ambitious programme, but most schools taught only the most basic work and concentrated on the 'three Rs' (reading, writing and 'rithmetic). Boys received some manual training, and girls were expected to learn cookery, housewifery, sewing, knitting and laundry.

The Dreaded Cane

Teachers used rigid discipline to encourage their pupils to learn, believing that the best way to govern was by fear. Girls and boys were made to sit bolt upright with very straight backs and arms folded on their desks in front of them. If they moved or whispered they were likely to be caned. A school cane was always in evidence, and even small children were beaten, most often on the hands, boys falling victim to such harsh treatment far more often than the girls. Soap was supposed to lessen the sting of the rod on the soft palms of the hand, and some lads, believing that they would be caned at least once during the day, would arrive in the morning with plenty of soap already rubbed in. Other boys used a different tactic, as Leonard Clark recalls: 'Some boys in my time believed that if a horse hair was wound round the palm of the hand it would render the cane impotent.' For more serious misdemeanors, the offending child was made to touch his toes and have his bottom caned. Some establishments were positively sadistic in their discipline.

A Change of Heart

To develop a more satisfactory and suitable education system, it was eventually recognized that national and local government must take a leading role in the organization and funding of schools. In 1902, Board Schools were abolished and local authorities took over control of elementary and secondary schools, set up an improved system of teacher training and granted subsidies to church and charity schools. The thinking behind the changes taking place was based on a new awareness of the needs of the child. Children were now seen as raw material to be shaped and moulded by parents and teachers under the careful supervision of the state. Gradually, the educationalists persuaded academics and politicians that children's needs were different from adults', and that schooling should include free play under the guidance of the teacher, gymnastic activities, handiwork, walks, poetry, story-telling, practical experiments, looking at pictures and listening to music, as well as reading, writing, arithmetic and more formal learning. There was a growing acceptance that it was unproductive to make the pupils sit behind their desks for hours on end

Classroom activities were still very formal and pupils were expected to work silently at their desks.

trying to concentrate on one task, that children could only apply themselves for a limited time, and therefore needed variety of pace and content during the day. Meanwhile, discussions rumbled on for several years as to whether school should offer a general education that built character and equipped students with accomplishments such as drawing, singing, appreciation of the arts as well as basic skills, or whether it should be biased more towards practical training that prepared each child for the kind of work he or she was likely later to become involved in.

Despite the changes in attitude the system did not, of course, change overnight. In many cases, schools continued on much the same lines as before. Victorian buildings continued to be used (and some are still in use today), but sanitation, heating and lighting were gradually modernized. Primary schools were divided into eight standards, each with its own master or mistress, and classes were of mixed ability. Arthur Newton recalls 'At the small age of three, I started attending Gayhurst Road School, London Fields. . . . At three years old the first class was more or less a nursery class. I remained at this school until I left to start work at fourteen. Classes were mixed in the infants, but boys and girls were separated from around eight or nine years of age. Classes were varied in size from approximately 30 plus, to as many as 50 in the higher standards. Subjects taught were chiefly reading, writing, arithmetic . . . geography, history, and in later standards

English, algebra, literature, art, handicraft (in the form of woodwork) and biology – chiefly concerned with the construction and function of the human body.' Similarly, Annie Wilson '. . . was just about three when I first went to school – the church school took you if you could speak plainly. . . . I went at nine o'clock and came back at twelve o'clock. It must have been three when we came home in the afternoon. There were odd teachers that I didn't seem to get on with at all . . . but I was so dead keen to learn. Good manners were most important. And to be truthful in all things. And tidy in your person. . . . We were all terrified of teachers.' A typical school day at Leonard Clark's school, as at others, started with 'four hundred strong boys in jerseys, girls in pinafores, with nine or ten teachers draped round the hall in various attitudes of reverence, the school would assemble for hymns, prayers and a homily from the Gaffer (the headmaster).' At A.L. Rowse's school, 'We assembled at nine o'clock, the school bell clanging harsh and more harshly out. . . . The Register was called, and we said "Present, Sir", or "Present, Miss". . . . Then we had prayers and a scripture lesson. . . .'

But teaching continued to be rather dull and uninspiring in many cases, and classes were still very big. A.L. Rowse says '. . . there was a lot of silent reading, it was called, during which our harrassed teachers with forty or fifty children on their hands would get on with their mark books or attendance registers while we read, more or less

*On the way to and
from school, or in
the dinner hour,
there was always
time for a game of
marbles.*

silently . . . .' Richard Church describes how 'Slowly and laboriously I learned the alphabet and the spelling of two-letter words, sing-songing them in a class of sixty infants following the red-tipped cardboard pointer in the teacher's hand, as she wrote the symbols on the blackboard.'

Bright children were used as teachers' helpers to work with the slower learners, so instead of forging ahead and learning more, capable students were held back. A child's progress to a higher standard was determined by ability rather than age, and students who reached the fifth standard were entitled to apply for a labour certificate which enabled them to leave school and start work at the age of thirteen. Some boys in special circumstances could leave before that, as Walter Greenwood explains: 'My headmaster was asking me questions at random such as what the product was of seven multiplied by nine. The quiz consti-tuted the "Labour Examination" ordained by the

Board of Education. It was open to fatherless boys who, if they passed, could finish schooling prematurely in order to go to work full time.' At fourteen, suitable boys and girls could enter for scholarships for entry to secondary schools, most of which were fee paying. Geoffrey Brady describes how '. . . my one chance was that I might get a scholarship. So at a very early age I was faced with the idea of slogging away at homework whether I liked it or not. . . .' He gained a place at a grammar school which was '. . . rather different from the county grammar schools; it was a very old foundation that went back to the 1400s, and apart from a few scholarships, you only got in if you passed good enough exams. . . . And so all the time I was at school I was pursued by this damned scholarship because if I skipped my homework or didn't do very well in one term . . . I might easily be sent for by the head.' But Geoffrey was the exception. Most working-class and lower-middle-class children educated at state schools did not go on to secondary schools.

New Methods of Teaching

Gradually, things did begin to change for the better. New elementary and secondary schools were built with modern equipment, teacher training improved and the number of available secondary places slowly grew. New buildings impressed young occupants with their spacious corridors, large halls with high ceilings and light airy classrooms. A.L. Rowse wrote that the new secondary school he attended was '. . . one of the girdle of schools built about the country as a result of the Education Act of 1902.' He remembers it with pleasure: '. . . we were that term 120 in number in buildings which were built to hold 200. So one had a great sense of space: empty classrooms unused, wide corridors, a staircase which we thought magnificent, an upper storey with windows giving on to the football field and looking out across the bay. It was very grand; one was impressed and happy from the first moment . . . you had a desk of your own, with books of your own provided by the County Education Committee. . . . The masters and mistresses, no longer plain teachers, wore gowns . . . and they changed with each lesson.' He really enjoyed his schooldays and wrote later: 'The school went along very happily and contentedly. . . . Hardly anybody was beaten; there was no need to resort to the cane. We were more like a happy family. I was very happy at school: I loved it.'

Teachers realized now that even if textbooks were still dull, oral lessons that were carefully prepared and well taught could awaken the pupils' interest and involve them in a way that 'silent reading' of required texts never could. New equipment and apparatus meant that science lessons could include practical experiments. Sport became a standard subject, and the classroom routine was more varied with regular trips to the local swimming baths, lessons in cricket and football, gymnastics and athletics.

Private Lessons

Lessons at home for wealthy children took place in the schoolroom with a private governess.

Only relatively small numbers of working-class children made their way through the new system of secondary education, and it was lower-middle-class pupils that benefited the most from the new opportunities. Wealthier middle-class and upper-class parents expected to pay for their children's education, and hired governesses and tutors for the youngest of their children. At the age of seven, boys were often sent off to private preparatory boarding schools ('prep' schools), while their sisters continued their studies at home or at exclusive day schools nearby.

Education began in the nursery, and it was Nanny who taught small children to read. Cynthia Asquith remembers 'It was sitting on Nannie's rather knobbly knee that, at a very early age, I learned to read from a chubby brown book called *Reading Without Tears*.' At five years old, infants left the nursery and Nanny's lessons to join the older children and the governess or tutor in the schoolroom. Governesses and tutors were not well paid, often receiving a lower salary than cooks and nannies, nor were they particularly well thought of, and since they did not enjoy very much respect or high status they tended to move on quickly from job to job. Some children thrived under their guidance and enjoyed their time in the schoolroom. Cynthia Asquith would later write: 'Because, I suppose, of these first enjoyable memories of lessons . . . the mere sight of a schoolroom with all its paraphernalia – ink-stained tablecloth, globe, wooden ruler, margined copy-books, neat time-table – is to me always a nostalgic sight.' Some middle-class parents, if they could not afford the full fee, would share the cost of hiring a governess and organized 'a little class'. Sybil Pearce was sent to a '. . . semi-private governess. She lived with her parents. . . . She constantly ate

oranges while she taught us and talked with a full mouth of the "Picts and Scots".... After the orange-history episode we had a reading lesson and then she gave up altogether and fell fast asleep.' Parents preferred to employ private teachers as they often considered day schools much too rough and unsuitable for their children. They were afraid that education in one of these establishments would involve a sort of intellectual and physical scramble with lower-class girls or boys, whereas, by bringing a governess into the home, parents could usually control the situation and guard against the wrong sort of influences. However, lessons went on without too much interference from parents.

In many cases, private teachers were good at their job and were respected and loved by their pupils. Katharine Chorley's parents found her a gem of a governess: 'Then Mademoiselle Dupuy came on the scene and for six years I was disciplined mentally, morally and physically in a way for which I cannot ever sufficiently say "thank you". Mademoiselle taught me everything except mathematics and English poetry, which Father supervised, and scripture which I learned from Mother.' Life in the schoolroom was disciplined and strict, and children were kept busy throughout the morning. In the afternoons, parents often sent their daughters for extra lessons in such subjects as riding and dancing at nearby academies and private schools. Rachel Ferguson '... attended classes for drill, dancing, French and drawing, with

a brief disastrous excursion into sewing and violin lessons.... Drill was held in the large glass-house which had a parquet floor, and save for Indian clubs, dum-bells, wands and skipping ropes, there was no apparatus whatever. Drawing also took place in the glass-house, and I, with a stout marbled book, laboured to reproduce laurel leaves and teacups.'

Away To School

After the first few years of lessons with a tutor or a governess in the schoolroom at home, wealthy little boys were sent away to 'prep' school at the age of seven, while their sisters continued their education with the governess at home, or were sent to private schools 'for the daughters of gentlemen'. At thirteen, boys and some girls moved to grammar schools or public boarding schools, and while boys finished their education at such establishments as Rugby or Eton, girls were often packed off to finishing schools in London or on the Continent to complete their training in deportment, dancing, music and art.

Children who were sent away to board found themselves alone for the first time in a strict and often hostile environment where each child had to fend for him or herself. Gervas Huxley recalls two pupils at his school '... who came the same term as I did and were removed by their parents after passing one or two terms almost constantly in tears.' Certainly the image of boarding schools was not a very tempting one, and Ruby Ferguson tells

The dining-room at Eton was a far cry from the cosy atmosphere of the nursery.

of the day her father said he was thinking of sending her brothers off to boarding school and organizing a governess for her. 'We all went green. "Oh Father! No, Father! Please, Father, no! Not that!" This was not surprising considering that all we knew about boarding schools had been gleaned from *Eric, Tom Brown's Schooldays*, and Dotheboys Hall (in *Nicholas Nickleby*). Father was a bit taken back by our shuddering reactions, but said, "All right, then. You'll go to the Polytechnic."' When older brothers and sisters did go off to school, their departure was a sad blow for the little ones left behind. C.S. Lewis described how '. . . my brother was removed from my life for the greatest part of every year. I remember well the rapture of homecoming for the holidays . . . I, meanwhile, was going on with my education at home; French and Latin from my mother and everything else from an excellent governess. . . .' Cynthia Asquith remembered, too: 'The worst of brothers was that they went away to school, leaving me in a house gone deadly quiet. No later leave-takings ever quite came up to the agony of those thrice-yearly seeings-off – eternal farewells they might as well have been. . . .'

A Harsh Routine

Boys often had to endure a much more rigorous routine than girls, with cold baths, fagging for the older boys, frequent bullying and very strict discipline as well as long hours of study and the essential dedication to activities on the playing fields. The harshness of the system puzzled some pupils, as Kenneth de Burgh Codrington remembers: 'It was not merely that I was bored. I had begun to realize that I did not really understand what was required of me. To get up, wash in icy water, run round the playground for a quarter of an hour, be prayed over twice daily and eat three sparse meals, to spend every afternoon in gladiatorial combat on the football field and most of the day learning things by heart, which meant very little to me, seemed to me to be an expensive waste of time.' C.S. Lewis was sent to a small private school which '. . . consisted of some eight or nine day-boys and about as many boarders. Organized games, except for endless rounders in the flinty playground, had long been moribund

and were finally abandoned. . . . The only stimulating element in the teaching consisted of a few well-used canes which hung on the green iron chimney piece of the single schoolroom.' Eric Gill experienced enormous dissatisfaction at the way subjects were taught, and later wrote: 'But I suppose few teachers in boys' preparatory schools in those days really wanted to teach. I suppose the great majority of them hated the job and were only doing it for lack of any other means of livelihood.'

At Rugby the boys had to get up at a quarter to six, take a cold bath and then attend one lesson before breakfast. At Harrow, as Henry Vigne recalls, 'In the morning you waited till the bell went for going up to chapel. You then leapt out of bed and you rushed downstairs to the basement and into a cold bath. You rushed upstairs drying yourself as you went, chucked some clothes on, went off to chapel which was, I think, at seven fifteen, as far as I remember, then you came back, had breakfast at nine. And I think the first school was at quarter to ten.'

Lessons involved a great deal of learning by heart. Latin was taught to even the youngest pupils and Greek was added later; in history they were given endless lists of Saxon kings and dates to learn; in geography the names of capital towns and rivers; English teachers taught grammar and how to parse a sentence, and set pupils the task of learning and reciting rather bad poetry. Gervas Huxley's experience of teaching '. . . in my first years was uninspired. It certainly failed to evoke any enthusiasm in me and I only worked at my lessons for fear of the punishments that were freely dealt out to delinquents.' These punishments included writing lines, staying in after class, canings and loss of privileges.

Sports and games were an extremely important part of school life. There was cricket in the summer and football or rugby in winter, as well as swimming, athletics and gymnastics. Some enjoyed the activity and showed real enthusiasm and commitment. While parents and teachers considered that the strict regime of lessons and sport was ideal training for the sort of positions in the Army and Navy and in the world of government, diplomacy and banking that upper-class and aristocratic boys would eventually take up. Rudyard Kipling wrote in *The Brushwood Boy*: 'Ten years at an English public school do not encourage dreaming. Georgie won his growth and chest measurements . . . under a system of cricket, football and paper chases from four to five days a week . . . the school was not encouraged to dwell on its emotions, but rather to keep in hard condition, to avoid false qualities. . . .' Others thought the emphasis on gentlemanly fair play and team spirit a hangover from Victorian days and out of touch with reality, but the obsession with team games and sports continued at many establishments.

Sundays gave the pupils some relaxation from study, but chapel and church services were compulsory, and students were expected to dress in their best clothes in order to do credit to the school. From their weekly pocket money they had to keep back at least one penny for the collection, and the remaining money could be spent later on sweets from the school tuck shop. After lunch there was free time when the boys would go for country walks, accompanied by a master, or parents might visit for the afternoon and take their sons or daughters out for tea. Katharine Chorley and her friends, at their seaside school, were marched '. . . up and down the leas winding in a decorous crocodile with a mistress at the tail among the strolling weekend visitors from London.'

There was a stark contrast between the comfort and security of home life and the almost prison-like atmosphere of school. From the time that mothers deposited their children on the first day of a new term through to the moment when they returned home to the warmth of the nursery and the companionship of brothers and sisters, children were often homesick and miserable. Gervas Huxley's life '. . . was divided into two wholly separate worlds. Six times a year I crossed the dividing line between them. Back at home I sought at once to bury school associations under the pleasure and comforts of my family life. Back at school I plunged into the routine of work and games so as to leave no time for vain home regrets.' At school, there was much to be endured. Older boys bullied and terrorized younger pupils with all manner of mean tricks – juniors were lined up and used as target practice for the older ones with their catapaults, wet towels were flicked at bare backs in dormitories, slippers were used to administer beatings, and cold water was poured into beds.

There was little privacy for the boys, and Herbert Read enjoyed '... no amenities – no private rooms, not even a reading room. A boy who wished to read a book outside class hours had to read it in the shrill pandemonium of the common playroom.' Henry Green wrote sadly: 'When we left our nursery, and the gardens or lumber room we could hide in, we found at school no corner even in the fields where we could be alone without having transgressed by being there, and that was something we were too afraid to do at first.' Kenneth de Burgh Codrington found the entire regime very difficult to bear: 'I could not get used to sleeping in a dormitory. Nor to the whispered conversations that were carried on after lights out. It seemed to me to be strange that the bluff, honest, open-minded English should leave their children in such ignorance and that

freedom-loving, individualist English should condemn their children to what amounted to a prison regime....' Herbert Read revealed that 'I have never lived under such a cloud of unhappiness as fell upon me once we had taken a brave farewell of our mother and the guardian uncle who had accompanied us on this first journey.' Duff Cooper admitted to '... doubts about the preparatory school system. It seems a cruel thing to take a child of nine away from his home and the loving care of his mother. ... I have known men who were spared the preparatory school or sent only to a day-school. I believe that they lost nothing and I know that they gained a few years of happiness.' However, he went on to say: 'In the life of an Englishman no period is more important than the years that he spends at a public school. He is a child when he goes there and he comes away a man. An older person takes him to the station when he sets forth for the first time, casting a regretful eye at the toy cupboard....'

A Kinder Regime

But not all schools and not all of school life was bad. Henry Vigne remembers being delivered into a master's charge at Victoria Station by his mother and he admits: 'I had a very cheerful time at school. I thoroughly enjoyed it. I remember feeling a bit upset you know just before the train left, but once I got there I liked it.' Gervas Huxley was sent to Rugby, and '... it seemed to me to be a most pleasantly adult place, where one's fellows

behaved with good sense and where one had far greater freedom than one had ever previously enjoyed. . . . Bullying or anything but the mildest form of ragging was completely unknown.' The rigid discipline certainly taught young children to stand on their own two feet and cope with any situation. Going away to school marked a sort of turning-point in the process of growing up. There

were new clothes, a new wooden trunk to carry possessions, new pens and pencils and a new adventure out into the big wide world. Moreover, schools took a much more humane attitude to the little children that were being handed into their care for almost forty weeks of the year.

New progressive schools had opened in the early years of the century and based their work on individual ability and value, respecting and encouraging each student's place in the school and in society, disabusing haughty individuals of ideas that certain things and people were beneath them, and determining individual progress by merit at work and not by character or wealth. Everyone was taught everything, including metalwork, acting and foreign languages; fagging was abolished; religion and sport played a much less important part, and teachers got on with the business of teaching. And in many cases, staff in quite ordinary schools organized extra activities after school so that underprivileged and less well-off children should enjoy the benefits that others took for granted. Florence Atherton explains: 'The teachers seemed to do a lot for us after school hours. Always something going on, socials, teaching us, going to school after school hours and showing us how to do things.' There were also more opportunities for girls, and it gradually became more usual for girls to stay on at school.

School Uniforms

Although elementary state schools did not usually insist on uniforms, private schools expected them to be worn. Herbert Read '... wore a uniform which consisted of grey trousers and waistcoat, an Eton jacket of blue facecloth, and a pork-pie cap with a straight flat peak of shiny black leather. In winter we carried grey Inverness capes.' At state secondary schools uniforms were usually worn, and A.L. Rowse '... set off downhill every

morning in the new-found glory of a school cap with a great many yellow ribbon rings around it and a badge in front, and with a satchel to carry my homework books in....' Girls' schools usually insisted on long navy or black skirts, black cashmere stockings, dark flannel blouses in winter and white flannel in summer. These blouses had long sleeves with buttoned cuffs, high collars that covered almost all the neck and were fastened with stiff ties. Even for tennis, lacrosse and cricket, and in the gymnasium, the girls had to wear tight, long-sleeves blouses under heavy, pleated gymslips. Katharine Chorley recalls that '... the clothing we wore impeded free movement for teachers and children alike. Most of the girls wore

On school outings, pupils were expected to walk in a tidy 'crocodile'.

76

"stays" and all wore long black stockings, as of course I did until shorter skirts came after 1918.' Cynthia Asquith's experience of physical training at '. . . McPherson's Gymnasium in Sloane Street was bliss. Exhilaratingly clad in blue serge tunic, a belt fastened with metal clips shaped like a snake, knickers and rubber-soled shoes, we marched, wielded Indian clubs, brandished dumb-bells, swung on parallel bars and vaulted over a contraption called the "horse"; all these activities carried on to the strains of "Daisy, Daisy, give me your answer do" and "O, Flo, why do you go, riding along on a motor car?"'

School Dinners

Some memories of school meals are of inedible food that left the children disgusted and hungry. Gervas Huxley recalls that the food at his boarding school '. . . was thoroughly bad. My stomach still turns at the thought of the breakfast porridge full of greenish sour-tasting lumps. The meat at lunch was generally considered to be horse. Between lunch and breakfast next morning, all we had was thick chunks of bread at tea, thinly buttered and with a scrape of jam.' Later he progressed to Rugby, where the boys lodged in a boarding house run by the housemaster. Here the food '. . . was of good quality, well-cooked and served, but as was

the custom, after supplying breakfast and lunch . . . bread, butter and tea were the only rations for the rest of the day, the boys being supposed to furnish any further eatables that they wanted such as potted meats, sardines and jam out of their own pockets.' State schools supplied meals for those that wanted them and were expected to recoup the cost from parents who could afford to pay. Thomas Morgan, who went to a school in the east end of London, writes: '. . . we mostly had our dinners at school. . . . The old milk churns . . . used to be delivered at the school full of soup. . . .' And Esther Stokes, at a Catholic day school in Clapham, south-west London, '. . . had lunch there and tea there. We had a presiding nun who said grace and who was in charge and . . . if we made too much noise, she'd ring a bell and say "Silence for the rest of the meal".' Ruby Ferguson's school impressed all the pupils and she writes 'I do not think that any school at the present day can be operating such an efficient food service as the Woolwich Polytechnic before the first World War. . . . The school was very advanced in the matter of food, as it served an excellent cafeteria lunch . . . the whole lunch was no more than sixpence.' That sixpence bought a choice of pork pie, sausage, poached egg on toast, fried fish, bread and butter, chips, cheese, pudding, cake, fresh fruit, tea, milk or lemonade.

PLEASURES AND PASTIMES

When lessons were over for the day, Edwardian children were never short of activities to fill their spare hours. If they were not playing outside in fields or gardens, they had a nursery full of toys and games to amuse them and all sorts of hobbies and pastimes to absorb them. Esther Stokes recalls that 'We played a lot of card games, 'cause that is a resource for a large family on a wet day, various forms of patience and simple bridge we played. I suppose whist. We never played chess – we played draughts and endless pencil and paper games that children loved, consequences and lists and telegrams. And then we loved charades. We were great ones for dressing up and playing charades at all special times.' Some hobbies, such as photography or riding, were expensive and demanded special equipment, but most indoor pastimes were accessible to all budgets and involved no great expense.

Cigarette Cards

The idea of including business and promotional cards in the packaging of retail goods originated in France in the first half of the nineteenth century. Retailers and merchants gave away cards bearing their name and address to encourage customers to return to them when in need of certain goods and services. So that they were not immediately thrown away, some companies decorated their cards with information and prints of relevant subjects, and the idea gradually evolved of printing sets of cards for customers to collect and keep. So,

Children loved to collect colourful cigarette cards that showed interesting activities and new inventions.

Edwardian children's books were filled with bright colourful illustrations to capture the imagination.

THE FIRST PNEUMATIC-TYRED BICYCLE

A NOTABLE TRICYCLIST— F. T. BIDLAKE

"ICIBLE" TANDEM TRICY

LADY CYCLIST WEARING DIVIDED SKIRT

the range of subjects depicted broadened to include fashion, wildlife, boxers, wrestlers, jockeys, soldiers – in fact any area of general interest. Boys and girls loved collecting the brightly-coloured cards from packets of tea or cigarettes and would rush to see what Mother's shopping expedition or Father's trip to the tobacconist's shop would yield.

Tobacco companies first included cards in cigarette packets in America in the 1870s, and in Britain in the late 1880s. By the 1900s collecting was a very popular hobby, and the range was extended further to include cars, motor bicycles, military uniforms and equipment, sports and sporting personalities, famous houses, beautiful women, actresses, famous explorers, autographs, Scottish clans, ships, wireless telegraphy, races of mankind, celebrated gateways, china and porcelain and characters from literature. Boys particularly liked the cards put out by Wills Cigarettes which depicted the heroes of the cricket pitch and the football field. Later, tennis and cycling also became extremely popular. Children stuck the cards into albums or special books that were printed by the card companies and which gave information on each page about the pictures and the objects shown. Gaps in collections were filled by organizing swaps or deals with friends and neighbours, and all sorts of games were played on floors and table tops in which one tried to win cards and build complete sets. As well as the standard cards, there were also novelty cards

which were highly prized. Some of these were made of metal or fabric, and some American tobacco cards had small celluloid buttons with pins on the back so that they could be worn as badges, or be attached to special souvenir cards.

Stamps

Stamp collecting started in England in 1841, one year after the first adhesive postage stamp was produced. The term 'philately' (from the Greek *Philos*, meaning love, and *atelein*, meaning without tax, because a stamp stuck on to a letter meant that it would be delivered without any further payment) came into existence in 1864 and was applied to the serious hobby of collecting and studying stamps. Before 1914, only a few tens of thousands of stamps had been issued around the world, and young collectors had a good chance of amassing an interesting album without feeling that there were still far too many stamps for him or her ever to dream of finding. Although 'classic' Victorian stamps were far too expensive for pocket money to buy, there were plenty of interesting examples to be had, either by buying from specialist dealers or by joining a stamp club. There were also specialist magazines which kept collectors in touch and sent stamps by mail order. An eager child arranged his or her stamps in a smart album that was organized in alphabetical order of countries and contained illustrations of special stamps. The best quality albums were covered with hand-tooled leather, and their pages

Scrapbooks

Making scrapbooks was mainly a girl's hobby, and while brothers organized their cards, rode into battle on toy horses or played with trains and cars, little girls of all ages sat quietly at the nursery table, or in the calm of their own bedrooms, and selected pictures from old birthday and Christmas cards, from magazines and from sheets of special pages of colourful scraps that could be bought in newspaper and toy shops. The children in Flora Thompson's *Lark Rise to Candleford* made their scrapbooks in the living-room. 'This room was the children's nursery. Their mother called it that sometimes when they had been cutting out pictures and left scraps of paper on the floor. "This room's nothing but a nursery," she would say, forgetting for the moment that the nurseries she had presided over in her pre-marriage days were usually held up by her as patterns of neatness.'

The carefully chosen pictures were lovingly arranged and then pasted into special books with blank pages. These were often in dull blues, greens, pinks and greys and were sometimes interleaved with protective sheets of tissue. Some books were expensively bound and had decorative title pages where the young owner's name could be written.

In the late eighteenth and early nineteenth century it was ladies and sometimes gentlemen who kept collections of verses, drawings, prose passages and oddments of information that were pasted into specially bound books. By the end of

Newsagents' windows were crammed with postcards and comics to tempt young customers.

were carefully separated by sheets of tissue paper to protect the prized collection.

Any child who had relatives who lived or holidayed abroad had the added advantage of acquiring unusual foreign stamps, and the postman's arrival every morning was awaited with great excitement and anticipation. What new issues would arrive stuck on to cards and letters from far away corners of the Empire, or from the Continent?

While little boys fought battles with tin soldiers, girls pasted scraps or mended favourite dolls' clothes.

the nineteenth century, scrapbooks had become mainly a child's pastime, and the range of scrapsheets included soldiers, ships, national costume, flowers, nursery rhymes, dogs, places of interest, fish, toys and letters of the alphabet. They were very brightly coloured and very appealing to the child's eye. Little girls could become thoroughly engrossed in the task of arranging the pages of their books with artistic displays of frocks and fans, flowers and gardens, Christmas figures or soldiers in all their different uniforms. Some children also saved old bus, tram or train tickets, price tags and mementoes from school outings. Postcards, photographs and bright labels from food tins and packets also made colourful displays. All that was needed was an empty scrapbook, a pair of scissors (not too sharp in case little fingers snipped too energetically) a pot of glue or homemade paste mixed from flour and water, and Nanny could leave her charges to amuse themselves quietly for hours. Some children even made their own Christmas and birthday cards by sticking suitable scraps on to stiff card. Parents and friends would have been delighted to receive such a simple but carefully- and lovingly-made gift.

Books and Magazines

Many of the favourite books of Edwardian children were written during the later days of Queen Victoria's reign. Boys' favourites were the adventure stories of George Alfred Henty, set during colonial campaigns and full of the deeds of young heroes. The tales of R.M. Ballantine, Robert Louis Stevenson, Captain Marryat and Rudyard Kipling were also very popular, and their dashing, rip-roaring tales of daring and adventure thrilled their young readers. Such tales of honour and patriotism were well suited to a time when the British Empire was at its peak.

Talbot Baines Reed was another widely read children's author, and the *The Fifth Form at St Dominic's*, written in 1882, remained popular well into the first years of the twentieth century. Charles Hamilton, writing under the pseudonym of Frank Richards, created Billy Bunter and his pals at Greyfriars to satisfy the demand for more school stories, and as the twentieth century progressed, stories gradually moved away from the 'blood and thunder' style of the Victorian tales of adventure with their moral issues and ideals of honour and gentlemanliness. The new style stories had a more grown-up flavour, but still appealed to younger boys as well as to their older brothers and sometimes even to their fathers.

Girls loved Charles Kingsley's *The Water Babies*, and George Macdonald's *At the Back of the North Wind*, *The Princess and Curdie* and *The Princess and the Goblins*. *Black Beauty*, *Peter Pan*, *The Wind in the Willows*, Beatrix Potter's *Tale of Peter Rabbit* and other stories, *The Secret Garden* and *Alice in Wonderland* were always well loved. Ruby Ferguson says: 'When anybody offered us a present we asked for books of a more expensive range like E. Nesbit, G.A Henty, and Rider Haggard stories, and once we got hold of Conan Doyle there was no stopping us from acquiring everything he had written. Then there was *The Children's Encyclopedia*, issued by Arthur Mee once a month, which we had to wrangle out of our pocket money as Father said it did us good to pay for what we wanted.'

Reading was encouraged by parents, and the time together in the late afternoon was often spent being read to by Mother. Herbert Read's mother '... read to us often, especially *Little Arthur's History of England*, *Evening at Home*, *Forget Me Not* and religious tracts such as *Little Meg's Children*.' And Diana Cooper recalled:

THE ...
GIRL'S OWN PAPER

'There was a lot of reading aloud and to oneself too. After *Stumps* and the *Pilgrim's Progress* there were fairy books in all their colours of red and blue, violet, yellow and even brown, with the imaginative Ford illustrations .... Next came

Girls' Own was really intended for young women, and many girls preferred to read copies of their brothers' Boys Own.

stories from Spenser's *Faerie Queene* and a book of Flaxman's drawings for the *Odyssey*, followed by Church's Homer and Kingsley's *Heroes* . . . . My Father's reading aloud *The Jungle Book* was a little beyond me, but being by a long way the youngest I was used to treading water and pretending to be cleverer than I was.'

Books were advertised by publishers as 'for the family circle' or 'for the fireside', and home reading was very much a group activity. But children also read alone in the privacy of their own bedroom or in the schoolroom or nursery. At school, too, much of the time was spent in silent reading. A.L. Rowse remembers becoming totally lost in his books in the classroom: 'How well I remember those somnolent afternoons: the hard benches without any backs, the difficulty of finding a comfortable posture and at length finding one, propping your head up with elbows on desk, hands over your ears so as not to be interrupted in your self-regarding pleasure.'

What made Edwardian books different from and more exciting than Victorian books was the wonderful illustrations. Books were designed to appeal to the child's imagination rather than merely to provide decoration. Walter Crane, Randolph Caldecott, Arthur Rackham and Kate Greenaway filled books with beautiful colour illustrations that drew the reader into the magic of the story, and involved them in the adventures and events of the fictional world. Parents, too, enjoyed the delights of the colour plates as they read aloud

to their offspring. They were glad that the young readers were attracted to books and encouraged them to occupy their minds with 'good' literature. At Christmas and for birthdays, popular gifts were *A Child's Garden of Verse*, *Tales from Shakespeare* and children's encyclopedias, which often included tales of courage and bravery as well as interesting and important facts.

Although parents generally disapproved of the weekly and monthly magazines and comics that appeared, most children loved them. Some of these were instructive and educational, and parents need not have worried since the stories in several of them, notably *Union Jack*, *Marvel* and *Boys' Own Paper*, were all of impeccable morality and the magazines did in fact help to encourage a great many children to read. The Victorians had called these journals 'Penny Dreadfuls', and the early Edwardians referred to them as 'Blood and Thunders', later abbreviated to 'Bloods'. *Boys Own Paper* included stories by George Henty and Talbot Baines Reed, as well as articles on cricket, swimming, making things, outdoor adventures and special offers of such items as stamps, magnifying lenses and lessons in handwriting. The magazine's ideal and aim was to combat evil by portraying goodness, honesty and decency as ordinary qualities. The editor from 1879 to 1912, George Andrew Hutchinson, had an extremely strong influence on British boys through his keen but unobtrusive emphasis on manliness and naturalness. He set high standards, but his standards

Comics and magazines offered a variety of fact and fiction, competitions and games.

class values into its stories. Heroes were upright and manly and always triumphant over rotters and cads. The characters in the adventures made ordinary school stories seem rather plain and dull. *The Boys' Friend* and *British Boys* had larger pages and were filled with serialized stories, instructions for making things, and hints about such things as how to become a policeman or a pilot.

As well as these classy magazines there were several cheaper periodicals of a much lower standard. Titles such as *Pluck* and *Comic Cuts*, containing lurid tales of burglars and tramps, used simple language and told several of their stories with pictures. But they were money makers, and children bought them, read them and swapped them for something more exciting. Younger children read *Young Folks' Paper*, which serialized simplified versions of such classic stories as *Treasure Island*, while *Chatterbox* was full of stories and activities. Gervas Huxley tells how 'On railway journeys we were sometimes given *The Strand Magazine* to look at, which, at that time, usually contained a brand new Sherlock Holmes story . . . . Our own travel-taste, however, ran more to highly coloured "comics" – *Ally Sloper's Half Holiday*, the *Rainbow*, etc. *Punch* was, of course, an institution in our house and we had the complete bound volumes from its start. These provided a really valuable background, even for my childish mind, to the whole social and political history of the Victorian age.'

were attainable by any ordinary, upright boy.

Chums was another good, wholesome and well-illustrated journal that was thought by many to be the best available. It stressed the merits of outdoor activities and incorporated good, solid middle-

Very little was published for girls, but they enjoyed reading their brothers' *Boys Own Paper*. Until *Girls' Own Paper* appeared, all that was available were trashy novelettes, full of silly love stories about aristocrats in their mansions. Ruby Ferguson recalls that 'The *Girls' Own Paper* was a highly popular publication, actually taken by Mother, because it was meant for older girls and young wives and contained love stories. I read it avidly, but the only thing I ever remember reading was an article called "How Two Girls Lived on a Pound a Week".' Some English girls subscribed to an American publication called *St Nicholas*, which was of excellent quality and was also popular with the boys. Working-class homes generally had fewer books and magazines than middle- or upper-class houses, but many families regularly took such weeklies as *The Leisure Hour, The Family Herald* and *Pears Cyclopaedia*. Richard Church says: 'The only journals in our home were the weekly *Titbits* and *Cycling* and the *Boys' Own Paper* and *Chatterbox*.' Whenever they could, poorer youngsters organized swaps with their friends and tried to lay their hands on as many back copies as possible.

Drawing and Sketching

Children have always loved to play with crayons and paints, and, as long as they did not make a dreadful mess, Nanny was quite happy for her charges to sit at the nursery table and play with their paintbox and brushes. Older girls were often sent to special private classes to learn how to draw and sketch, as these were still seen as essential female accomplishments. Their little sisters were happy to daub bright patterns and attempt portraits of Mother and Father until they too were old enough to attend classes. Gwen Raverat's drawing class was taken out '. . . to draw buildings and streets and animals, and we learnt about architecture and perspective and anatomy. . . . From the age of nine, when the Drawing Class began, I always kept a sketchbook going, and drew everything I saw. They were bad drawings; still, I suppose I learnt something from the habit, – observation, if nothing else.'

Dressing Up

Dressing in fancy clothes and playing at 'Let's Pretend' is another timeless pleasure for all children, and most Edwardian bedrooms, nurseries and playrooms had their dressing-up box or basket. Diana Cooper tells how 'At home we had the feather-and-flower box, the ribbon-and lace drawer, the fur chest (very mothy), the stuffs – yard upon yard of dress lengths for all times and seasons, plushes and chiffons, sprigged muslin and cloth of gold. All these precious reserves in time found their gay end in the dressing-up box, a huge wicker hamper, a cornucopia spilling out skirts and hats, a few yellow plaits for Wagner, helmets, swords, ballet-shoes, deer-stalkers, boas, Ophelia's straws and flowers, jackboots, wimples and wigs.' Laura in *Lark Rise to Candleford* had a blissful time one day in her cousins' attic, discovering the joys of dressing in discarded clothes: 'Dressed in apron and shawl, the point of the latter trailing on the ground behind her, she gave her best imitation of Queenie, an old neighbour.... Then, draped in an old lace curtain for veil, with a feather duster for bouquet, she became a bride.'

Some children preferred to act their plays out through puppets and dolls. Ruby Ferguson recalls: 'We had made ourselves a theatre, painted the scenery, sewn the curtains and everything worked. For a penny or two we were able to buy from the Penny Bazaar sheets of cut-out cardboard characters for various plays which we acted in full, reading all the parts, to any captive audience we could collect.'

Carefully sewn new clothes kept favourite dolls in current fashions.

Middle-class children usually learnt to play a musical instrument and often performed at family gatherings.

Musical Boxes and Gramophones

Most upper-class children, particularly girls, were expected to learn to play the piano and sometimes other instruments, but since this was regarded as part of their education it was often not a pleasurable hobby, but rather a chore or a duty. Some time each day was set aside for lessons and for practice, and afternoons and evenings were sometimes spent playing music together in the drawing-room. As pure entertainment, musical boxes gave far more pleasure and children would open and close the lids to hear again and again the tinkling magic. Rachel Ferguson remembers '... my box played "The Man who Broke the Bank" and bore

a blurred picture of a man fishing from a punt. I don't suppose it cost half a crown.' Herbert Read's father '... brought home a delightful toy from Northallerton: it was a small musical box which played "For there's nae luck about the house" ... Mariana was fair as sunlight and smiled to the tinkle of the musical box.'

The first phonograph had been produced in 1877 by Thomas Edison, and in 1887 Alexander Graham Bell introduced an improved version, the graphophone, using wax cylinders which eventually were adapted to bring recordings of popular songs into the home. A little later in the same year, the first gramophone was introduced, and its flat discs produced a much better sound quality. By the

The gramophone brought the highlights of the concert stage into the home.

early 1900s, the machine had been refined and improved and wealthy families could afford to buy one for their drawing-rooms. Some children enjoyed the music downstairs, while other very lucky ones had their own gramophone up in the nursery. Madge Hodson and her sisters had one upstairs and, since Harry Lauder was a great favourite of their nanny's, over the years they heard quite a number of his songs. But the machine did not reach the majority of homes until after the First World War, by which time it was regarded as an adult toy rather than a child's plaything.

Magic Lanterns

Magic lanterns date back to the early nineteenth century, when burning lime provided the rather hazardous light source. By the end of the century, electricity was more widely used for commercial shows, but most machines used in the home were lit by oil or paraffin lamps. It was often on winter Sunday afternoons that families would gather in the dining-room, waiting in excited anticipation while one of the men assembled all the complicated pieces of the machine. Then they sat spellbound in the flickering darkness while images of Punch and Judy or scenes at a zoo illuminated one wall. Early slides were large and cumbersome, framed in heavy mahogany, but as technology improved so the slides became easier to handle and more interesting and varied in subject matter. Favourites were slapstick comedies, nursery tales, scenes of the countryside or views of famous towns and castles. As photography developed, slides impressed their audiences with enthralling melodramas and hilarious comedies that were acted out by real people.

Other Indoor Pursuits

Boys spent much of their time playing with model trains and cars, and organizing sets of tin soldiers into battle formation on bedroom floors and table tops. Some also ventured into magic or amateur chemistry while their sisters played with their china dolls, rag dolls or paper cut-out dolls and their versatile wardrobes of clothes for all occasions. Girls also learnt to knit and crochet, among

other things, as Diana Cooper recalled: 'The piano was practised, drawing and clay modelling were encouraged as a game, and we would sew and embroider in wools and silks and ribbons, making our dreadful Christmas presents of sachets and velvet holders of shot to act as my father's paperweights.'

For any spare moments, there were stocks of board games, jigsaws and packs of cards that had been given as presents or bought with carefully-saved pennies. Dominoes, ludo, snakes and ladders, spillikins, tiddly-winks and lotto were as popular then as they are today. Happy Families, Patience or Snap were played with as much enthusiasm and noise as would be seen and heard in any modern playroom. But, if the weather was dry and warm, Nanny or Mother encouraged the children out of the nursery and into the garden so that lungs could be filled with fresh air and young limbs could stretch and exercise.

Modelling with plasticine was a good activity for rainy days.

OUT IN THE FRESH AIR

On a fine day, there was nothing better for Edwardian children than being out in the open air. Working-class children were sent out in all weathers to occupy themselves in streets and country lanes, while on cold, blustery days, more privileged youngsters played in their warm nurseries. But when the sun shone, everyone looked forward to playing out in gardens and fields, exploring woodlands, bicycling along country lanes, fishing in streams and ponds and turning paths into marbles pitches and roads into football grounds. Flora Thompson writes: 'After they reached school-going age, the boys no longer played with the girls, but found themselves a separate pitch on which to play marbles or spin tops or kick an old tin about by way of a football. Or they would hunt in couples along the hedgerows, shooting at birds with their catapults, climbing trees, or looking for birds' nests, mushrooms, or chestnuts, according to the season.' There was an infinite range of activities to fill the days, and children were reluctant, at dusk, to give up their adventuring and games of chasing, hopscotch and skipping, and make their way indoors again, for tea and bed.

What could be more fun than flying a kite on a windy day by the seaside?

Collector's Items

Then as now, during trips to the seaside all boys and girls loved searching for shells. It was great fun to tear off shoes and socks and to paddle along the shore and in rock pools hunting for pretty cockles, winkles, whelks and razor shells. The shells were washed and treasured in boxes, or used to decorate picture frames or jewellery boxes, or arranged into ornate designs and mounted in a frame. Children liked to copy the designs they saw on boxes and frames in the seaside souvenir shops. And little shells were indispensable when playing shops – they made tempting sweets and cakes on the toyshop counter, or became valuable currency that paid for the delicacies.

Birds' eggs were popular with adults and children alike, and it was a perfectly acceptable hobby in those days to raid nests, blow out the egg and preserve the shell as a decorative item to be displayed on shelves and in glass cabinets. Herbert Read describes how he became involved in this hobby: '. . . I wandered with my cousin, a boy five or six years older than myself. He was a keen collector of birds' eggs, butterflies and flowers, and had a great cunning in the pursuit of these objects.

Edwardian children loved collecting birds' eggs.

From him I learnt how to handle birds' eggs, to empty them through one blow hole, to pack them in match boxes! We carried catapults and I was taught the honour of the chase. Which birds it was legitimate to shoot, how many eggs one could take from a nest, how to rob a nest without spoiling it or discouraging the mother-bird.... Sometimes we would be out all day, regardless of meals. We gathered wild gooseberries and stewed them in a tin over a fire of twigs.'

Amateur Snapshots

For nature lovers, the advance of the camera added a new dimension to their forays into woods and pastures. Before 1890, photography was an activity practised by professionals, and not generally understood by lay people. But technical advances during the early 1900s made portable cameras more available, and meant that amateur photographers could have a go for themselves. Taking a photograph no longer involved huge pieces of equipment, tripods, bottles and chemicals. Modern photographic paper and light-weight box cameras allowed the keen photographer to record the activities of family and friends, and wild life, and portable cameras could easily be carried on bicycling trips or excursions by tram or car and used to capture images of children playing by a stream, of ladies in long skirts wobbling along on their cycles, or of families enjoying a picnic. Favourite pictures were mounted in ornate albums with decorated leather or velvet covers.

Children would have had to save hard to be able to buy all the necessary equipment for this expensive hobby. Cameras were not cheap and the actual processing of the film would have demanded a sizeable collection of Saturday pennies, but more privileged children were often given cameras, films and albums so that they could practise their skills and record their success in their own collections. Philippa, in *The Fortunes of Philippa*, combined birds'-nesting with trying out her new camera: 'I had had a kodak for my last birthday

Before offering home developing kits, Kodak's slogan had been 'You press the button, we do the rest.'

present, and I was anxious to take some snap-shots of the young birds in their nests, fired thereto by the beautiful nature photographs I had seen in the illustrated papers. With a good deal of climbing and difficulty I managed to secure various views of Mrs Thrush at home, Mrs Chaffinch's nursery, and five Miss Hedge-sparrows clamouring for a meal.'

Fun on Wheels

Wheels were an important part of Edwardian playtime, and if no bicycle was to be had, then home-made carts, old perambulators and barrow boxes on wheels were used for hurtling down hills. But bicycles were much better, and as they became cheaper and more widely available, everyone wanted one. It did not matter if it was a brand new Raleigh or a well-used and decrepit bone-shaker: as long as it worked, it would do. Sybil Pearce remembers her early days in the saddle: 'A great event now was learning to ride a bicycle. I was not given a bicycle, I had to hire a second-hand one from the cycle shop . . . for sixpence an hour. My father held the back of the saddle while I rocked and gyrated up and down. . . . After this I had a second-hand bicycle bought for me which had been done up and repainted and which gave me the freedom of the world.'

Some parents would not allow their children to ride cycles, as they considered them unsafe, but most youngsters had a machine which provided endless hours of adventure and fun, and offered a quick and easy means of transport to school. Before the days of such cheap mobility, many rural children had to walk miles to school every morning and home again in the afternoon. In the late 1880s, Flora Thompson explains, 'Cycling was looked upon as a passing craze and the cyclists in their tight navy knickerbocker suits and pillbox caps with the badge of their club in front were regarded as figures of fun. None of those in the

Bicycles gave children the freedom to explore and adventure in the nearby countryside.

hamlet who rushed out to their gates to see one pass . . . would have believed, if they had been told, that in a few years there would be at least one bicycle in every one of their houses, that the men would ride to work on them. . . . They would have been still more incredulous had they been told that many of them would live to see every child of school age in the hamlet provided by a kind County Council with a bicycle on which they would ride to school, "all free, gratis, and for nothing" . . .' David Garnett rode to school every day on an old

*Home-made carts and barrows were
excellent substitutes for bicycles and toy cars.*

Bantam, '... a diminutive variety of the old
ordinary or penny-farthing high bicycle', the type
of cycle which had been fashionable in the mid
1880s.

Most children saw their bicycles as a passport to
freedom. Geoffrey Brady '... was always fond of
cycling. I had an ancient rusty old bicycle at a fairly
early age. . . . I used to go off by myself on my bike
for half a day or get some sandwiches and go off
for the day sometimes. And cycling was a good
deal safer than it is now, but on the other hand the
roads were totally different and after five miles
you were simply white with dust from head to
foot.' W. MacQueen Pope recalls: 'And it was a
very pleasant exercise indeed, in those seemingly
distant, quiet and peaceful days. . . . One was
carefree, death did not lurk at every corner, at
every crossing. There was space, there was room,
there was freedom.' And if the children were not
allowed to venture far from the garden or estate,
they rode their cycles there. Esther Stokes
remembers '... lovely wide gravel paths ... which
were great fun for cycling. We used to race round
them playing all sorts of bicycling games.'

Out in the Garden

Children were often given their own little plot of
garden to look after, and some spent hours
tending and weeding, and chatting to the family
gardener, begging for advice and for seeds and
plants to grow. Esther Stokes had 'a big garden
with clipped hedges and formal rose beds and a

The children's plot was dug and watered as carefully as the rest of the garden.

tennis court. And we all had a little plot of our own, stone flagged so we were supposed to look after it, some of us were keen and some not so keen, planting things like love-in-the-mist. . . .' When not digging and sowing, the children played. Gervas Huxley writes that gardens '. . . were a source of endless pleasure to us children . . . our chief recreation was a swing in a piece of wild garden where blue convolvulus rioted up a bank. . . . We also had a lair in a thick patch of shrubbery where there was a tangle of hops which we used as food in our games of keeping house.' To Herbert Read, 'The front garden was an annexe of the drawing-room, and not part of our customary world', but he did have a sand pit which was '. . . a generous heap, allowing an extensive system of trenches and castles; near-by was the shade of the apple trees and the elms; our days there were timeless. Once, playing there, I slipped into the cow-shed to stroke a young calf housed there, closing the door behind me. The calf was lying in fresh, clean straw, and did not stir at my approach. Hours later, I was missed and after long searching and much shouting in the farm and fields, I was discovered sleeping with my head against the calf's warm flank.'

Sticklebacks and Trout

Very little equipment was needed for a fishing trip, and children without proper rods created a makeshift rod from a branch and a piece of string or wire. Then they could sit beside lakes and rivers waiting to hook minnows and sticklebacks and pop them into the waiting jam jars that sat ready on the grass. Walter Greenwood tells of 'Spring-time, when small boys put away their whips and tops and, with half-penny fishing nets and glass jam jars, risked a hearty whack across the backside from a park-keeper's stick while lost, at the duck pond, in the absorbing hunt for sticklebacks brilliant with love's gorgeous and transient livery.'

Serious and well-heeled young fishermen set off with proper rods and bait to try and entice bream and perch on to the hooks laced with flies and worms. Madge Hodson tells how her father taught her to fish in the lake in their family estate, and how she and her brothers learned to catch trout. Rudyard Kipling's *Puck of Pook's Hill* conjures up the freedom and pleasures of the countryside for the children during the hot idle days of summer: 'They were fishing a few days later, in the bed of a brook that for centuries had cut deep into the soft valley soil. The trees closing overhead made long tunnels through which the sunshine worked in blobs and patches. Down in the tunnels were bars of sand and gravel, old roots and trunks covered with moss and painted red by the irony water. . . . This was one of the children's most secret hunting grounds. Except for the click

of a rod hitting a low willow, or a switch and tussle among the young ash-leaves as a line hung up for the minute, nobody in the hot pasture could have guessed what game was going on among the trouts below the banks.'

Heroes of the Sports Field

Sports were very important to Edwardian children, and in an age when the British were champions at football, golf, rowing, tennis, cricket and athletics, most schoolchildren enjoyed playing one or more of those popular games and had sporting heroes whom they worshipped. The King himself, though not a cricketing or footballing man, took a great interest, and he was actively involved in sailing and horse racing. Cricket caught the

Cricket was so popular that major advertisers often used the image of the young batsman to sell their goods.

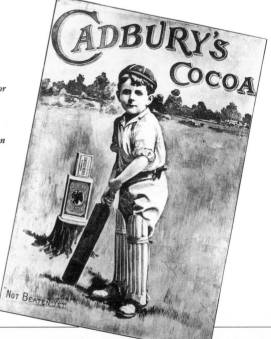

attention of many young lads, their interest perhaps stemming from early matches on the cricket pitches of their prep schools and public schools, where the game was taken very seriously. Some schools employed professional county players as coaches in order to improve standards, and 'house matches' were played between the different houses within a school, as well as matches between rival schools.

Team games were treated almost as a cult that was closely linked to the Empire building of the Victorian age. The rigours of sporting activities were believed to be character-building and to teach self-discipline. The boys were encouraged to play with dedication and enthusiasm, and they followed national and county matches with as much passion and fervour as went into school tournaments. Matches in those days were exciting, with fast action, plenty of runs and attractive personalities to thrill the crowds. Neville Cardus wrote: 'During the whole of the summer of 1902 I seem to have lived free as the wind watching and playing cricket . . .. Long days at the county ground, full length on the grass. And every evening we would go forth to the fields and play on bare dusty earth until the sun went down and you had to crouch at the stumps like Jessop to see the ball against the reddening sight-screen of the sky.' For a small boy the importance of the matches was overwhelming.

Eric Gill was another avid follower and recalled seeing his hero, Ranjitsinhji at the Sussex country cricket ground in Hove, of whom he wrote: 'There were many minor stars, each with his special and beloved technique, but nothing on earth could approach the special quality of "Ranji's" batting and fielding.' Other favourite players were W.G. Grace, C.B. Fry, Sir Jack Hobbs and Wilfred Rhodes. Boys read about their stars in newspapers, and cut out reports of matches to stick into scrapbooks or hide away in boxes of personal treasures. They also collected cigarette cards that depicted the major personalities, and many practised hard at school to improve their own skills. Cynthia Asquith tells how her brother '. . . was such a keen cricketer that when we were children he used to practise bowling at me by the hour. One day, when for some reason we were confined to our London house, I remember his bowling me out sixty times with an apple. A fire shovel was my bat; the coal scuttle our wicket.' Every keen young player's ambition was to possess his own bat, and the advice given in *Boys' Own Paper* and similar magazines as to the washing, oiling, sanding and storing of the vital piece of willow was carefully followed.

Rugby football, hockey and tennis were also taken very seriously at the public schools. Association football, although played at many leading public schools, was also very much a working-class sport and was played at the state schools. Town children spent hours kicking a ball around the streets between makeshift goalposts made out of sticks or cast-off jerseys. Sometimes the girls joined in a game of five-a-side football – even if there were six or twenty-five children, it was always called five-a-side. The boys spent spare moments collecting, swapping and playing with cigarette cards which depicted their heroes, and they loved Saturday afternoons when fathers, uncles and brothers took them off to watch a match at the local stadium.

Boy Scouts and Girl Guides

The Boy Scout movement was born in 1904 when Lord Baden-Powell, veteran of the Boer War, started organizing trips for boys from the towns into the fresh air of the countryside in order to develop their skills of observation and to allow them to enjoy the freedom of the outdoor life. The organization did not really take off on a large scale until 1907, when 'B-P', as he was known, set up the first Scout camp on Brownsea Island in Poole Harbour, Hampshire. He wanted to test his new ideas before going ahead with a wider movement. His idea was to devise games and activities to be played in the open air, away from school and the sports field, in order to train young minds and educate youngsters for responsible citizenship and service to the community. He laid great emphasis on religious toleration, outdoor activities, the need to help one's fellow men, an appreciation of nature, fun and spontaneity, a freer approach to children and a need to break down class barriers.

B-P wanted to attract boys from all kinds of backgrounds, and so he did not just invite the sons of his public school acquaintances and friends to Brownsea. He approached the local Boys' Brigade in Hampshire and asked if they were interested in sending a few boys to join the camp. Eventually, a group of twenty boys – ten from London, seven from Bournemouth and three from Poole – arrived on the island for a week of hut- and mat-making, knotting, fire-lighting, cooking, endurance tests, boat management, woodcraft, the study of stars, plants and animals, health and sanitation, life-saving and games.

In 1908 B-P published *Scouting for Boys*, a collection of stories, games, tips and advice, which initially appeared as six fortnightly parts at a price of 4d each. As this was quite expensive, groups of boys pooled their resources and rushed out to buy shared copies. They could hardly wait for the first edition of the *Scout* magazine, a weekly newspaper that first appeared on 18 April 1908. Boys everywhere, and from all backgrounds, were inspired by B-P's ideas on adventuring, war games, tracking and doing good turns. Groups met wherever they could – in cellars, in halls, in each other's houses – and sent off for registration forms from headquarters in London. They also had to find willing men to be their scout masters.

Many people were suspicious of the Scout movement at first, thinking that the idea was to lead young lads into military training. As B-P's career had been in the Army, these sceptics thought he was trying to build a junior militia. The movement was also seen as a rival to Sunday

No. 1. Vol. 1. APRIL 18, 1908. PRICE ONE PENNY.

THE SCOUT

FOUNDED BY
GEN. BADEN-POWELL

THE EVENING MEAL

Copies of the first edition of The Scout *were snapped up by boys all over Britain.*

Cooking on a wood fire was one of many important skills learnt by Boy Scouts.

School, and some parents would not hear of their children missing church.

For boys that were allowed to join, training was very serious, and tests of observation, skill and judgement were undertaken with enthusiasm and commitment. Field days were organized, and boys were given first aid instruction and tested on it. Henry Green described how 'We used to go out and earn badges for lighting one fire with not more than three matches, and I remember how strange it felt to be trusted with anything so dangerous. Later, having got the badge for lighting fires, we boiled potatoes in billy cans to get cooking badges.' On one occasion, 'I fell down and hurt my knee, so they tied scarves across two scout poles in the way it is laid down in regulations and tried to carry me back.'

The movement grew so rapidly that district committees and local associations were set up to co-ordinate troop activities. A second camp was organized in 1908, and in 1909 a huge rally was held at Crystal palace. Although girls were not yet involved, the first group of self-organized female Scouts, not wanting to be left out, made an appearance at the rally dressed in an improvised uniform of blue skirts, white blouses and black stockings. B-P realized that the girls needed to be included, and his sister Agnes took on responsibility for the newly-formed Girl Guides. By the end of 1910 there were nearly 108,000 Scouts and Guides in Britain, and groups were also being formed in other parts of the Empire and in Europe. In 1913, a programme for junior Scouts was laid down, and in 1914 a scheme was outlined. Because of the Scouts' close links with Rudyard Kipling, the ideas for this junior body sprang from *The Jungle Book*, and the first display of the Cubs was given on 16 December 1916.

Leapfrog was a favourite game and kept the children warm on cold days.

Horse-Riding and Hunting

Most children from wealthy families learnt to ride at a very early age. Henry Green tells how '. . . as soon as my two brothers and I grew long-legged enough to get a grip of the saddle we were put up on ponies and taken out hunting by a groom on leading strings.' Cynthia Asquith's first ride was '. . . an immensely solemn affair. Long-tailed, thick eye-lashed, a shetland pony, round as a barrel, scarcely higher than a dog, and wedged into a high basket saddle, the absurd small proud bundle that was myself uneasily perched on that broad swaying back.' For Gervas Huxley and many others like him, 'Regular riding lessons were also part of our curriculum. We started at an indoor riding school and later used to join a party, led by a riding master, that walked, trotted and cantered in Rotten Row.'

Herbert Read remembers following the hunt on foot when he was too young to ride: 'My father rode one of his beautiful hunters; my mother had her pony. At first we children went on foot as far as the Covert and saw them take off, and piped our tally-ho's if we caught sight of the fox. . . . But when I was seven I was given my first pony, and then rode away with the hounds.'

Outdoor Fun and Games

Children did not need expensive toys to enjoy and amuse themselves in Edwardian days. Out in the street or in the garden they invented their own fun. As Flora Thompson wrote, 'In winter, their

little limbs purple-mottled with cold, they stamped around playing horses or engines. In summer they would make mud pies in the dust. . . . If they fell down or hurt themselves in any other way, they did not run indoors for comfort, for they knew that all they would get would be "Sarves ye right. You should've looked where you wer' a-goin'!"' The children were quite happy 'outlining houses with scraps of broken crockery and furnishing them with moss and stones; or lying on their stomachs in the dust to peer down deep

All that was needed for fun in the river was a simple shrimping net.

cracks dry weather always produced in the stiff clayey soil; or making snow men or sliding on puddles in winter.' Henry Vigne says: 'I think all our amusements were what they call home-made. Roller skating was a great thing of course . . . at prep school. We had a lovely concrete area we used to skate and play hockey and all sorts of games on skates, great fun.'

In summer there were streams and rivers to swim in, and hedgerows to be explored. And, as Patricia Lynch writes, 'When we weren't in school, or exploring, or helping Mrs Foley, who was the washer woman for Fair Hill, and it wasn't raining, or time to go to bed, we played in the yard.' In that yard or out in the streets, tops were whipped into action and hoops were bowled with sticks. Some played with skipping ropes, balls, marbles and five stones, while others played hopscotch, leapfrog or ring-a-roses. Girls skipped backwards and for-wards, to rhymes and songs, with arms straight or arms crossed. They skipped two jumps to a turn or two turns to a jump and they played running-in games while two others turned the rope. Marbles were rolled and won and lost. Flora Thompson explains: 'Marbles, peg-tops, skipping-ropes appeared in their season, and when there hap-pened to be a ball available a game called Tip-it was played. There was not always a ball to be had; for the smallest rubber one cost a penny, and pennies were scarce. Even marbles, at twenty a penny, were seldom bought, although there were a good many in circulation, for the hamlet boys

Wealthy children learned to ride as soon as they were big enough to sit astride a small pony.

Muffins and crumpets were tea-time treats in winter.

were champion marble players and thought nothing of walking five miles on a Saturday to play with the boys of other villages and replenish their own store with their winnings.'

Marbles were played during Lent. After a summer of swimming, cricket and fishing, the autumn was heralded by games with conkers. Hoops were a winter toy, as Richard Church explains: 'With the coming of cold weather, iron hoops were heard trundling to school, driven by boys with an iron hook in a wooden handle.' As the weather grew colder, frozen ponds and lakes became skating rinks and slides, while snowy slopes were toboggan runs. Diana Cooper tells 'We were chiefly at Belvoir [her grandfather's castle in Leicestershire] in winter, I suppose, for I think of the tobogganing down slopes worthy of a world's fair, and my fear of the horse-pond ice breaking and drowning Letty, and of day and night prayers for snow.'

Throughout the year, gangs of boys tormented householders with their games of 'knock down ginger', which involved knocking on doors and then running away before anybody had a chance to see who was there. Sometimes a piece of string was tied between two adjoining door knockers, so that as one lady opened her front door, her neighbour came scurrying to see what was going on. Another favourite trick was to startle old ladies with 'whizz-bangs' – small explosive bags that went off with a very loud retort when thrown hard on to the pavement.

But not all children were involved in such naughtiness. Most played on home-made seesaws or swings and played chanting games and hand-clapping games that had pretty tunes. 'Here We Go Round the Mulberry Bush', 'In and Out the Dusty Bluebells' and 'Oranges and Lemons' were all favourites. And for chasing games a counting out rhyme was always used to find who was 'it', the chaser. Hide and Seek, What's the Time Mr

An ice slide was just one of the joys of winter playtimes.

Wolf?, Grandmother's Footsteps and others were played with shrieks of mock terror as one child sought to catch or find the others. Gwen Raverat played 'hide-and-seek out of doors at night; the party was divided into two sides, and a lantern was placed in the middle of the lawn, to be Home. Tiptoeing about in the rustling blackness of the garden, with a potential enemy behind every bush, was altogether too much for my nerves though, of course, I dared not say so.'

Boys and girls often joined together to play 'Have You Seen the Muffin Man?' One boy stood in the middle of a circle formed by all the players, while everybody sang, 'Have you seen the muffin man who lives down Drury Lane?' The boy then chose a girl who replied, 'Yes I've seen the muffin man who lives down Drury Lane.' The whole circle then sang, 'Oh two have seen the muffin man who lives down Drury Lane'. The two then danced and chose two new partners. The game continued until everyone was dancing.

Occasionally, while the game was going on on a winter Sunday afternoon, the real muffin man would arrive, carrying a tray of freshly-baked muffins on his head and ringing a bell to warn of his arrival. Or perhaps the 'windmill' lady or man would appear with a bundle of coloured twirling windmills on sticks. For a few rags or jam jars, a child could buy one of these prized toys, so the game would be broken up and children would scatter in all directions to go and see if their mothers could find something to swap. Or, sometimes a family with a barrel organ and a monkey would slowly make their way up the street begging for a few pennies, or a bear on a chain lumbered after its owner, standing up on hind legs to beg for cash. Once these entertainments had moved on, the games were resumed, and little groups of children returned to the marbles scattered in the gutter, or started turning the skipping rope again to chants of 'Salt, Mustard, Vinegar, Pepper', and the street would resound once more with the rattle of an old tin can as little feet in well-worn shoes tried to score another goal.

A VISIT TO THE TOYSHOP

Most children were given pocket money each week and saved the pennies in a money box. When the tin weighed heavily enough, the precious savings would be tipped out and taken to the toy shop to be exchanged for a box of soldiers, a mechanical boat, a doll or a teddy bear. Walter Greenwood recalls: 'For us who were young, Saturday was the crown of the week. "Spending money" was in our hands, the "Saturday halfpenny" given with the warning "And,

think on, you're not to spend it all at once."' Geoffrey Brady's '... pocket money was a penny, literally a Saturday penny .... You could buy a quarter of sweets for a penny.' Even poorer children managed to earn and save little hoards of pennies, as Clifford Hills explains: 'I had a grandmother alive in those early days and she used

William Brittain's toy soldiers were tied into a straw- board box before leaving the factory.

Children chose carefully from the treasures of the toyshop before spending their few pennies.

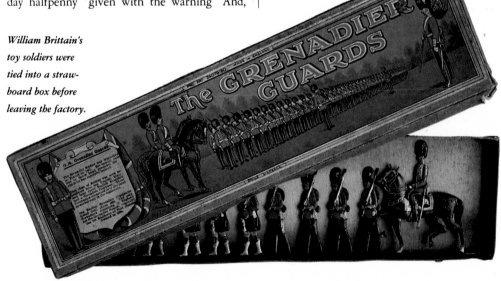

American cast-iron money banks that quickly conveyed pennies from hand to mouth.

to save my pennies and we were always earning pennies, we'd go around trying to earn pennies somehow, even searching the local pond for a beer bottle and get a penny on it ... and my grandmother used to save all the pennies, put them in a handkerchief, put them in her pocket in her old dress underneath her pinny, and she didn't tell me how much I'd got till I went to the Sunday School treat. And I remember once I had four shillings and I thought I was a millionaire.'

All boys and girls saved their pennies very carefully, for Nanny and parents impressed upon them the importance of thrift. Money boxes were made to be as attractive as possible in order to encourage children to save. Tins and boxes came in all shapes and sizes. There were cheap pottery ones and bright red tin plate pillar boxes. There were bright pink pigs, symbolic of the family pig, which was a great investment and was killed to

provide winter food and sometimes even mortgaged to ensure supplies of other family requirements. Hens on nests guarding their eggs likewise emphasized the need to plan ahead for a rainy day. Cheap cast-iron and tin were used to make milk churns, pears, rabbits, barrels, treasure chests, books, cottages and castles. From America came mechanical boxes with moving figures that relayed the pennies to a slot, or that reacted with some special action when the penny dropped into the box. From France came a model vending machine that rewarded the child with a chocolate when a penny was invested, and from Germany, where most tin plate mechanical toys were manufactured, came acrobats, bucking horses, mules, Punch and Judy shows, a barrel organ with a monkey that danced, and shop tills that rang a bell as they registered the deposit. Some had musical boxes as part of the mechanism and responded to the saving with a tune. Sharps sold their toffees and Huntley and Palmer sold their biscuits in tins shaped like houses or telephone kiosks that could be used as money boxes when all the goodies had been eaten. Bright colours and the imaginative shapes made money boxes toys in themselves, and they provided amusement for their young owners as well as encouraging them to think to the future.

When the 'piggy bank' contained enough pennies, a child could make the magical trip to the local toy shop and choose from a vast array of mechanical toys, dolls, train sets and games. Most of the toys produced during the early years of the twentieth century were very well made and tended to last for a good number of years. There was something for everyone, rich or poor, and the greatest problem was how to choose from the display on the shop shelves. Rachel Ferguson recalls that 'The Teddington toy-shop was good, but the one at Kingston was unique. For Pulborough's was small, bow-windowed, and if I remember, one step down, and a bell on the door that tinkled. It was kept as is meet and right by an old lady, and was most certainly lamp-lit. On winter evenings it was fairyland, a marvel-muddle of glittering cheapness and a drawer bursting with penny toys.'

Rag and Porcelain Dolls

Until the end of the nineteenth century, wax was the most popular material for making dolls, and London wax doll makers ran very successful businesses. The dolls often represented smiling round-faced children and were cheap enough for all but the very poor to buy. Simple muslin bodies were filled with straw, and some had wigs implanted into the scalp. The moulded legs had black or orange boots painted on to the wax, and more wax was then brushed over to soften the effects of the paint. In 1901, Lucy Peck ran a 'Dolls' Home' in Regent Street, where high-quality model wax dolls were manufactured, and where children could take their old wax dolls in order to have real hair fixed in place. Pecks was the only manufacturer of the period to use a wired-eye mechanism that allowed the doll's eyes to move. Eyeballs had a layer of wax painted over them to make them more life-like.

In America during the 1890s, hundreds of advertising dolls were made to promote cottons, dyes and coffee, while, in Britain, Barbour's Irish Flax Thread was promoted by a series of figures dressed in costumes based on flowers and fruits. Sunlight Soap also gave away dolls, and German breakfast foods were advertised with cut-out figures. Many of these dolls took their place in Edwardian toy cupboards alongside the more elaborate baby figures and rag dolls that had also been popular since their introduction in the 1880s. The favourite, Betty Blue, appeared in 1910 – 'From the top of her head to the soles of her dainty brown shoes, Betty Blue is indeed a darling dolly.' Most rag dolls were stuffed with wood-wool or cork so that they could be washed.

The best china was always set and everyone was dressed in their finest for a dolls' tea party.

At the beginning of the twentieth century, porcelain dolls were increasing in popularity. Early porcelain heads were mass produced in Germany, and were attached to sawdust-filled fabric bodies. Gradually, processes were developed whereby white bisque (a type of porcelain fired to the biscuit stage and left unglazed) that was left over from production in the French and German porcelain factories, was used to make the dolls' heads. Flesh tones were added, fashionable hair styles were fixed in place and jointed arms and legs, made from the same material, were attached. The resulting dolls were very life-like, and the chubby infants continued to be popular until the 1920s. In Edwardian times, the most sought-after version, cherished by many little girls, had sleeping eyes and curly hair. Cheaper types had moulded hair, coarse fabric bodies and arms and legs that were rather too small for the rest of the body. Some had glass eyes and small flowers or combs moulded into the hair, and rings, bracelets and earrings applied to fingers, arms and ears before firing. Some were sold undressed, with bodies made from novelty fabrics that showed the American flag or geometric designs.

As bisque dolls were fragile and broke easily when dropped, companies experimented with other, more durable materials such as rubber, celluloid and metal, but bisque continued to be the most successful and the most popular. French manufacturers produced a hard composition body made from a mixture of whitening, resin and glue that was moulded over wire frames and which gave the dolls a more life-like appearance.

In the early years of the twentieth century, a new interest in child psychology led manufacturers to wonder about the child's emotional involvement with its toys and playthings. Some doll makers thought that the chubby, idealized babies with their sleeping eyes and real hair were too perfect and left no room for the child's imagination to work. So, in 1904, the Dresden craft shops asked designers to supply ideas for more traditional dolls that showed character and personality. As these became available, retailers were highly suspicious and worried that they would not be able to sell them, but hundreds of little girls and their parents started ordering and buying them, and the new dolls in their bright costumes became a huge success. The dolls were, in the advertisers' jargon, 'Full of individuality and character and yet always remaining childish, so true-hearted and bright, so charmingly pert and rakish.' These 'character dolls' had bisque heads, composition bodies and bent arms and legs, with one arm bending towards the body. The eyes were painted, the mouth was slightly open, and the features far more realistic than those of the idealized dolls of the late nineteenth and early twentieth century. Some manufacturers even filled the bodies with enough sand to give the doll the same weight as a real baby.

But this trend for character dolls was short-lived and the new craze in 1907–8 was for 'caricature dolls' who had amusing expressions and unusual features. 'Goo-goos' and 'Googlies' had whimsical expressions and moving eyes that were operated by a string in the back of the head. Kewpies appeared in 1912 and were made in the form of chubby children with large heads and quiffs of hair standing up from the forehead. Each doll had a sweet expression, a very round tummy and small wings sprouting from the shoulder blades. The legs were moulded together, the arms were outstretched and the hands were webbed. The huge googlie eyes made them enormously appealing and over five million were sold.

With the development of the phonograph came talking and singing dolls. Simple talking mechanisms that said 'Mamma' or 'Papa' had been used since 1884–5, but in the early 1900s, tiny versions of the phonograph were fixed into dolls' stomachs so that they could sing several favourite songs to amuse their young owners.

But not every child was lucky enough to possess an up-to-the-minute doll, and old favourites had a special place in the hearts of many small children.

Nannies, mothers, sisters and aunties all did their bit to repair old clothes, and make new ones so that Dolly at least looked fashionable. Sybil Pearce remembers an old favourite: 'I had one large doll called Beryl dressed by a clever dress-maker Aunt of mine called Auntie Bo-Bo. She took as much pride in my "baby" as I did. . . . Poor Beryl! I took her paddling in the sea and her papier mâché feet disintegrated; but her lovely auburn hair still remained beautiful.' Sybil had a smart pram for Beryl and she tells how 'I used to be allowed to take out my doll's perambulator. . . . It was a charming perambulator – a honey coloured basket-work body with shafts to push it by and a white linen canopy edged with lace.'

Mechanical toys delighted Edwardian children with their attractive appearance and clever actions.

The Doll's House

One corner of most Edwardian nurseries was filled by a doll's house, and most girls and some boys found enormous pleasure in entering this magic world of make believe. It didn't really matter if it was an expensive mansion or a modest home-made dwelling, hours of fun were to be had in organizing the furniture, arranging the vases and candlesticks, the toys and the kitchen utensils, and

As long as their dolls had a home, little girls did not mind if it was simple or grand.

moving the people that lived there from one room to another as they gave instructions to their servants or made sure that their children were behaving themselves up in the nursery. Freya Stark recalls 'a doll's house my father built out of boxes, swinging open with all its doors and windows and muslin curtains attached, and closing again on the dolls within, who seemed alive but less comprehensible than people or animals.'

Most doll's houses were made as detached town houses and reflected urban life. As many were imported from Germany, along with the miniature furnishings, both exteriors and interiors were often Germanic in style, but sometimes paper façades were stuck on to give the appearance of English villas or mansions that were usually more Victorian than Edwardian. However, modern trends were reflected by the installation of bathrooms, and lifts to carry baggage and residents from entrance hall to top floor, and Edwardian taste in interior design was evident in the amount of Chinoiserie furnishings and fabrics, and in furniture inspired by the style of William Morris and other Arts and Crafts designers. Some houses even had a garage for the new motor car, and the most expensive had running hot water and lavatories that actually flushed. For small bedrooms and nurseries, fold-away houses were made in sections that could be dismantled when not in use.

Since most wax, bisque and rag dolls were much too large to live in these miniature residences, tiny china dolls were made to scale, and had a very happy time rolling pastry in the large, well-ordered kitchens, relaxing in rocking-chairs and armchairs, or playing in nurseries and school-rooms, among the usual supply of blackboards, games, cradles and dolls.

As well as houses for dolls to live in, toy shops also sold dolls' clothes and all the paraphernalia that any self-respecting doll could possibly want. Rachel Ferguson tells how '. . . after tea, we strolled to the toy shop . . . where mother bought

me a box of doll's note-paper in lovable shades of pink, green, peach, blue and buff, "because we weren't very good at our lessons, today".' Rachel also tells how 'On another birthday, Mother's presents were a doll's dinner table, laid even unto midget napkins in metal rings, and a draper's shop, fitted up with tiny hats, a good ribbon department, and on the shelves . . . Manchester goods.' Shops stocked tea sets, hair-brushes, bathroom sets, cooking pots and pans, and all these miniature pieces of equipment were as popular then as they are today. But there were many other wonderful toys to catch the children's attention and charm intrigued young shoppers.

The President's Teddy Bear

The first teddy bears made their appearance in the toy shops in 1902. Although a German company, Margarette Steiff, had been producing bears since 1897, the sudden popularity of the bear in Britain and America resulted from an incident in the United States when President Theodore (Teddy) Roosevelt, while out on a hunting trip in Missis-sippi, refused to shoot a tiny bear cub. The press, of course, made as much as they could of the event, and a cartoon by Clifford Berryman of the *Washington Post* depicted Teddy's Bear. Another American, Morris Michton, founder of the Ideal Toy Corporation, had started producing small toy bears earlier in 1902 and was responsible for adopting the President's nickname for the new fluffy creature. By 1904, huge numbers of bears from Britain and Germany were competing for a place in every child's toy collection. Until teddy bears arrived, there were very few soft cuddly toys, and children adored having one of these new, fluffy fellows to play with and to take to bed. In *Summoned by Bells*, John Betjeman tells how he lay in his nursery bed

And turned to Archibald, my safe old bear,
Whose woollen eyes looked sad or glad at me,
Whose ample forehead I could wet with tears,
Whose half-moon ears received my confidence,
Who made me laugh, who never let me down.
I used to wait for hours to see him move,
Convinced that he could breathe.

*The actress Ethel
Oliver with an early
golliwog.*

The early bears were not the big-eared chubby animals of today, but had rather long arms, pointed snouts, humps on their backs and glass eyes. Claws and mouth were embroidered in black thread, and pads of leather, felt or leathercloth were stitched on to the soft mohair body to make paws. They were stuffed with kapok, sawdust, wood-wool, straw or cork granules, and the fur was usually golden in colour, although black, dark brown and even red were available. Arms, head and legs were movable, and the projecting muzzle was very realistic. They were made in all sizes from two inches to several feet high, and in 1909 Peak Freans used a group of foot-high furry bears to promote their newly-launched Teddy Bear nursery biscuits. In 1910, one company made a white, female bear called Barbara, but she was never a success. Meanwhile, the male bear infiltrated every aspect of nursery life. Cups, saucers, plates, mugs and tea sets appeared bearing pictures of teddies, toy shops stocked candle holders, puppets, building bricks, musical boxes and money boxes all decorated with bears, while furniture and wallpapers added their versions of the popular toy to nursery and bedroom decor. The toys were dressed up in uniforms, in smart bow ties or ribbons; they were undressed, brushed, taken for walks, cuddled, given tea parties, taken to bed and generally doted upon. Long after children had outgrown their other toys, Teddy still occupied pride of place on the nursery bed, or he travelled to school or later to a new home.

Golliwogs

The first golliwog was a character in books by Florence Upton, published in 1895 about two Dutch dolls and a 'golliwogg'. The popularity of the funny black toy, which appeared in the early 1900s, reflected the strange taste of the time for black toys.

The soft toy was a huge success with its rag or sawdust-filled body, its black face, embroidered features and hair made from loops of wool. He usually wore a neat Eton collar, bow tie, brightly-coloured coat and smart trousers. Although he was generally a much-loved playmate not all parents approved. Diana Cooper's mother could not abide him: '... tolerant of toys, she was unsympathetic to any that were conventional or comic. Japanese dolls and Japanese crinkly-paper books were encouraged. She abhored anything in the fashionable golliwog style.'

The Wonder of the Tin Toy

One of the greatest innovations in the world of toys at the beginning of the twentieth century was the tin toy. Germany led the field in toy manufacturing, and from 1895 onwards production expanded rapidly thanks to technical advances and to the introduction of mass production using tin plate, most of which came from South Wales. A great deal of care and thought went into the design and manufacture of steam and clockwork boats, funnel liners, submarines, gunboats, battleships, carriages, and clockwork figures such as barbers

Colourful circus acts were popular subjects for clockwork tin-plate toys.

rubbing cream into customers' scalps, violinists, butchers chopping meat, men pulling carts and goose-stepping soldiers. The range was vast. To make such appealing and attractive toys, the shape was first pressed out in tin plate and then soldered together. Each toy was carefully tested before being hand-painted and then fired to set the enamel. Some were then finished with an air-brush spray, and, before being released from the production line, were tested again very thoroughly to check that all the moving parts were working. The toys were then packed into wooden boxes filled with wood shavings to protect the delicate mechanisms during transportation to the toy shop. Some of the toys were very sophisticated and had elaborate working parts that were set in motion by clockwork, rubber bands, steam, hand cranking, gravity, electricity, flywheels, compressed air or gas contained in special cylinders. Steam boats really did have wheels turned by steam; and airships, balloons and dirigibles really did float through the air. Because all these toys reflected contemporary life, they had a particular appeal for children, and their parents were often delighted to buy such amusing and attractive toys.

Many of the toys were intended to cause laughter. 'Tut-tut' was a car driven by an erratic driver of questionable skill who blew a little horn as the car zig-zagged around the room. A lady riding in a horseless carriage tried with her umbrella to shoo away a dog that had jumped on to the running board. And Rachel Ferguson recalls, 'In the Teddington nursery of our friends the Foxes was a mechanical model of "Joe" Chamberlain. . . . When wound, Joe hurried about the floor, making as much sustained progress in any direction as was, unhappily, to be the case at Munich.'

Some of the toys were less well put together, and were not meant to last. The intention was to provide cheap and colourful entertainment to suit all pockets. Many of the novelty figures produced between 1895 and 1914 cost only a penny, and children could choose between fire engines, donkeys and carts, dogs, horses, nannies pushing prams, clowns doing acrobatics, balloonists, jugglers, drunkards trying not to lose their balance, performing elephants, tight-rope walkers, removal vans with a stock of packing cases, milk floats with milk churns, farm carts with sacks of

produce, railway vans and push-along vendors' carts with fruit and vegetables, bread and confectionary. Gamages Catalogue for 1910 shows metal sedan chairs, crawling beetles and walking crocodiles, cockerels pulling little carts, horse-drawn and horseless carriages, delivery vans, merry-go-rounds, dancing couples, magicians, railway porters and tricycle carts. Toy cars were extremely popular, the first ever being produced by Rossignol, a French company who made a toy Renault taxi in 1905. New models were quickly manufactured to keep pace with new fashions in the motoring world and some even had windows made of bevelled glass and doors that opened. Ships were equally successful and could perform quite complicated manoeuvres – imagine the fun at bath time with a battleship or ocean-going liner being torpedoed by a sneaky little submarine that hid beneath the bubbles!

Toy Trains

Toy trains had been favourite playthings ever since steam revolutionized the transport system in the 1830s. Early train sets were made of wood or metal and were played with ceaselessly by Victorian boys. Clockwork trains, first produced in America in 1856, provoked more excitement, and when model steam engines that really worked appeared in the early 1890s, countless little boys must have pressed their noses covetously against toy shop windows, wishing that someone would buy them one for Christmas. They were not to know that just a few years later, in 1897, the first electrically-powered train set would appear in America, and that European companies would follow suit in 1898. Model railways evolved a complete system with stations and signals, carriages, passengers and baggage, and an entire network of rails and points that could, and sometimes did, take over the entire nursery. Fathers, of course, often became just as involved as their sons in devising elaborate routes across bedroom floors and around nursery furniture. Home-made trains could be built out of Meccano with sets introduced in 1901, but most little boys wanted to own the real thing, with the beautifully-crafted carriages and the powerful engines that pulled the little trains so smoothly.

Model Armies

Early tin soldiers were manufactured in Britain by Britain's Ltd in 1893. The hollowcast models were made in a brass mould into which molten lead was poured. The resulting soldiers were a very accurate representation of British soldiers in their various uniforms. They had movable arms and flesh-coloured faces, and the painted details of the face and the uniform were of a very high standard. The sets of soldiers were sold in boxes made of strawboard, and then distributed to shops on the Continent as well as in Britain. By 1907 more than a hundred different military units were offered, with tents, guns, tanks and forts for the model fighting force. The Boer War, the arms race with Germany and the spread of amateur war-gaming

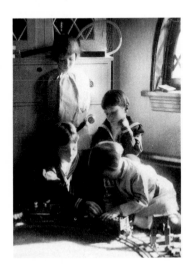

Little boys spent hours playing with treasured train sets.

117

in such movements as the Boy Scouts led to an increasing interest in miniature armies, and German and French manufacturers also started producing vast quantities. The Germans quickly dominated the market with a huge variety of inexpensive infantry, rifle regiments, fusiliers, foot guards, Highland regiments, hussars, dragoons, lancers, cavalry, cowboys, Red Indians and foreign troops.

A Rich Selection

As well as all the teddy bears, dolls, tin toys and soldiers, an infinite selection of games and other toys awaited wide-eyed customers in the toy shop. Many of the best-selling toys and games were exactly the same as had tempted Victorian children. There was no abrupt change in variety or in taste – there were still Noah's Arks (one of the most popular toys of the late nineteenth century), jigsaws, games of ludo, snakes and ladders, tiddlywinks, draughts, spillikins, skittles, wooden and stone building bricks, spinning tops, hoops and marbles. The latter were made of marble, clay or stone rather than glass, and they sold at twenty for a penny. Glass ones were rare and much prized by the lucky boys and girls who were given them or who won them in contests.

Skipping ropes cost a few pence and hoops varied from 6d to 1/-. Hoops were still well-loved and children spent hours trying to master the art of keeping them rolling. Sybil Pearce recalls that 'Another joy at this time was my wooden hoop

Toy soldiers were even more fun when they had a great castle to guard.

and stick. Mother would carry a camp stool down on to the Green and place herself in the shade and I would endeavour to bowl my hoop, guiding it with the stick. It was intended that the hoop should be bowled along in a straight line and never allowed to wobble from side to side. This feat I

simply could not manage. It wobbled and stalled and fell flat to the ground every half yard.' Spinning tops sold for a halfpenny each, so even poor families could afford to buy one from a shop or travelling pedlar. Twirlers were spun between thumb and forefinger; teetotums, made of wood or ivory, were used like dice in games that groups of children could play together; and wooden peg tops were tossed to the ground from a tightly-

With a nursery full of books, games and toys, there was always something interesting to do.

wound string that sent them whirling across the road or floor. Whoever's top spun for the longest was the winner. The metal tip helped the top to endure the bumps and bangs it received as it landed and spun on the stony ground. Whipping tops were set spinning with a long leather whip that was used from time to time to keep up the momentum. Some tops were brightly coloured so that they produced a kaleidoscope effect as they spun, and humming tops made of chromium-

the century weren't ninety-five per cent more likeable and attractive than any made since, with (to me) the sole exception of the pedal motorcar that came too late for me to possess. . . . Certain Old Crusteds of the toy-box persisted in every era, bricks, dolls, dolls' houses, wooden rifles and pistols, most of which bored me. . . . But where in all England would you find today those chunky little booklets which, when whirred over the thumb, showed the photographs within in action?

The nursery was a haven where favourite toys filled dreams and adventures.

plated steel sang to the children as they revolved gaily on the floor. Rachel Ferguson speaks of a '. . . lantern affair slotted with silhouettes which, when spun, gave the effect of movement, and the large tin top which, when spun, gave fourth what sounded like the organist practising on Saturday evening in the village church.'

Rachel Ferguson goes on to say: 'I challenge any contemporary to deny that the toys of the turn of

. . . Where would you find the Bavarian village in which, at the turning of a handle, the villagers filed past to a tinkling tune and vanished down a slot? This could only have cost a few shillings, or my brother could never have given it to me. And where are those loops of green chip to which was attached red cotton and a small skeleton which, when the loops were compressed, turned somersaults?' The toy shops were crammed with card games, spelling games, bagatelle, bowls, bingo, magic sets, kites, kaleidoscopes, shuttlecocks and battledores, table tennis bats and celluloid balls, jack-in-the-boxes, musical boxes, miniature domestic equipment for little girls so that they could cook, wash and sew to their heart's content. There were cameras and educational toys that helped with numbers and letters; there were little play houses, miniature furniture and household equipment. Rachel Ferguson had '. . . a full-sized hut with hinged windows, and capable at a pinch of holding myself and three adults for tea. . . .' The hut was set up in the garden, and '. . . on winter nights it was wonderfully cosy, cramped and warm.' Then there were the bicycles, the tricycle-carts, the horses on wheels, the rocking-horses with manes of real horse hair, and the model cars. Looking back, C.Day Lewis admitted: 'All through childhood, I longed passionately for a pedal motorcar and importunately hinted at my need for it: but no pedal motorcar arrived. I received many noble presents but I remained faithful to a battered bear called Bouncer who was like a brother to me.'

The toy shop was indeed an Aladdin's cave of treasures, and to be allowed to spend an enchanted hour or two gazing at the colourful display and perhaps choosing small purchases was a real treat. Ruby Ferguson remembers visiting Gamages when it first opened: 'It was heaven. We meandered from department to department feeling like travellers in exotic lands who had stumbled into a cave of treasures. Two hours went like a flash. Paul finally settled for a kodak which took his whole five shillings, and with his birthday money, saved up, he added some of the necessary equipment.' The Edwardian years were truly the Golden Age of toys and playthings, and many children like Ruby and her brother spent happy hours dreaming their way past shelf upon laden shelf of soft cuddly toys, pretty dolls and exciting games, and wishing that it was their birthday or Christmas tomorrow, or that they had saved just a few more pennies in that precious money box.

OCCASIONAL TREATS

Whatever class or background an Edwardian child was from, the daily routine of meal-times, lessons and play was brightened by occasional treats. Some were quite small – a new toy or an extra piece of cake at tea-time. Others were really special events that remained in the memory for many years. An expensive new outfit for a birthday party or a day a trip to the zoo or a big museum, or an afternoon's shopping with Mother – all created an interesting diversion from the ordinary round of events. diversion from the ordinary round of events.

Cynthia Asquith's life was liberally scattered with small treats: 'As well as indoor delights, there were manifold "going-out-with Mamma" treats. Tip-toed, heart-beating explorations of the mysterious dark wood of yew trees that skirted the magnolia lawn and was said to be the headquarters of a dragon. Tea, or reading aloud under the great shimmering green parasol of the tulip tree; inspection of the round pond in the kitchen garden to see whether the gold fish were still orange coloured.'

As Gervas Huxley recalls, 'Treats varied our routine. Some Sunday afternoons we were taken to the zoo, on others we visited one or other of the South Kensington museums.' And Geoffrey Brady, of Manchester, tells how 'We used to go to Belle Vue regularly. Belle Vue in those days was much more of a zoological garden and less of a general sort of entertainment place . . . they used to have great firework displays.' For many children the most special event of the early 1900s was the King's coronation, for which all sorts of treats and entertainments had been planned. Unfortunately, the king fell ill with appendicitis and all the celebrations had to be postponed.

Every town in Britain planned elaborate celebrations for the coronation of Edward and Alexandra.

All sorts of craft were used for family outings on the river.

A Shopping Trip

Most children loved the bustle and activity of town centres, and a trip with Nanny or Mother to the big shops was cause for great excitement. First, there was the thrill of the journey by horsedrawn carriage, tram, train or motor car. Cynthia Asquith enjoyed the fun of travelling around London by public transport: 'Four-wheelers – "growlers", as they were called – I did not like. . . . Hansom cabs – the gondolas of London, as someone called those gayest of conveyances – I have never ceased to regret. I loved their jauntiness, the jingle of the bells on the horse's head, and the way the doors closed across my legs like a wooden apron.'

For Sybil Pearce, too, it was the journey that held the greatest attraction: 'Some of my favourite days were those on which my mother decided to go "up to town" shopping. We would catch a two-horse drawn omnibus in the Bath Road . . . and my great joy was to seat myself just behind the driver on the top of the bus in the front seat. It took us an hour to get to Queen's Road, Bayswater – where we shopped at Whiteleys. . . . If it rained we were covered with black mackintosh covers lined with tartan, which, when placed over me, came up under my chin.'

On arrival at the correct destination there was the hubbub of the busy streets with carriages, trams and people everywhere. Rachel Ferguson recalls the danger of London traffic in those days: '. . . crossing Piccadilly Circus then was, to a country-bred child, exactly as alarming as it is now to anybody, for carts, hansoms and horse-drawn omnibuses came at one from every direction.' Once inside the shops, there were elevators gliding from one floor to another, magically transporting excited shoppers from one department to the next, there were counters laid out with enticing displays of all sorts of unimagined objects, and smart assistants just waiting to serve eager customers. Stephen Potter recalls the exhilaration of his shopping trips: 'Going to London to shop with Mother . . . meant not only the complex experience of the Army and Navy Stores, which always included at the very least, a long stare at the train section of the Toy Department, a long smell in the leather goods, a long stew in the splendidly fearful odours of the menageries and a melting visit to the Sweet Department to buy Pyramid Creams – a sweet so delicious that I had to try not to think of it on ordinary days; it meant also a drive up in the Victoria tram. Electric trams had the dignity of newness then – there were still horse trams on view.'

Shopping trips almost invariably involved going somewhere for tea once all the packages had been secured. Marie Condie of Glasgow remembers: 'I went with my grandma to Anderson's Polytechnic for shopping, for clothes and household things an' that. Then we always went to Ferguson's for a pot of tea and a cake . . . I loved that.' And Cynthia Asquith recalls a winter tea which was 'one of those occasions when a drop of real tea was put into your cup of milk.' Then she was taken home – 'With a gingerbread-nut popped into my mouth to "keep out the cold", a leather strap buckled round my middle to secure me to the back seat of the four-wheeled dog-cart, and my legs packed into a fur-lined bag.'

Museums and Exhibitions

Visits to London and large towns were sometimes made in order to spend time in museums and historical places of interest, such as the Tower of London or Westminster Abbey. The large London museums, built during Victoria's reign, were as popular with children and adults in the Edwardian era as they are today, and although the exhibits were not as excitingly organized as they are now, they were highly regarded by teachers and parents for their educational value, and loved by fascinated children for the novelty of such things as prehistoric monsters, scientific inventions and models of the planets.

Permanent exhibitions were also open to the public at Earls Court, built in 1887, at the White City, Shepherd's Bush, and at Crystal Palace. Earls Court staged the Austrian and Hungarian Exhibitions in 1906, and the Golden West Exhibition in 1909. These were excellent for giving information about foreign countries and cultures, and were favourite rendez-vous for all classes, including Royalty. From the West End of London, the journey by train or bus took only a few minutes, and once there, as well as the actual exhibitions of art, engineering, ceramics, metalwork and minerals from the countries concerned, there were amusements, side shows, tea on the lawns, promenades and frivolities. Between 1 p.m. and 11 p.m., bands played in the different corners of the grounds, and around the gardens were distorting mirrors, haunted castles and water chutes. Sybil Pearce was enthralled by '. . . a land of fairy lights, gay music and cream toffee made – while you waited – on a silver spit. What delicious nights they were! You sat on little green iron chairs listening to the band and as the summer evening breezes blew up you huddled near to Mother who had brought her fur cape for warmth. Coming home was lovely too, only one was too sleepy to realize the beauties as one passed the jewelry stalls all alight with gay beads on elastic and the cries of the girls and boys on the water chute.'

For Cynthia Asquith the Earls Court Amusement Park was '. . . exactly my idea of Paradise. . . . The switchback was good enough (its climax of the double dip made even the phlegmatic shriek) but the water chute! That really was ecstasy . . . the rapturous suspense of the slow stammering ascent, the at first stealthy downward glide instantaneously accelerating into a breathtaking swish through the air. Down, down, down, shot the boat, until with a gigantic slap it struck the surface of the water and bounded off it high into the air.'

The White City opened with the Franco-British Exhibition in 1908. It had all the features of Earls Court, but was larger and even grander, and was designed in a new style of architecture with domes

*The Franco–British
exhibition at The
White City in 1908.*

*The streets of the
big cities were
thronged with
motor and horse-
drawn vehicles of
all descriptions.*

and minarets. The enormous grounds covered an area about a mile long and a third of a mile wide. The entry fee was one shilling, which gave unlimited access to eleven palaces with their displays of art, music, machinery and textiles. Around the grounds there were cascades of water, bands playing, a scenic railway, fairground rides, a big wheel called a Flip-Flap, and all night the entire area was illuminated by over one million multi-coloured electric bulbs. The tube line from the West End was extended to carry people to the Exhibition ground for a fare of twopence, and the White City became extremely popular with the working classes as well as with upper-class people and royalty. Queen Alexandra is said to have particularly liked the scenic railway.

Rachel Ferguson's family took her to all the favourite places: 'Gaps in the social round were filled by Ranelagh, Hurlingham, Earls Court Exhibition and the White City, Shepherd's Bush. The latter, created by the brothers Kiralfy, was as consumedly dull as Wembley was to prove, and for much the same reason; that for the distance to be covered the side shows were exiguous. But Earls Court was a lovable outing, compact, varied, pretty and a godsend to the after-dinner party.'

Other large towns sometimes had their own annual extravaganzas. David Marriott of Glasgow remembers: '. . . it came year after year for a long time. There was this big arena wi' clowns and jugglers, acrobats an' that. But the last turn was what you really waited for. Before it started, they put up a big high splash screen all round, with scenery of woods and waterfalls, except at the entrance. Then someway or other the floor sank down and water gushed in, then Indians in canoes came scooshing through, like they were shootin' rapids.'

All the Fun of the Fair

Travelling exhibitions and fairgrounds brought entertainment and amusements to those living too far from London to be able to enjoy all those major attractions of the metropolis. Fairs and shows often arrived for Bank Holiday weekends when working people had a day free from work, and could indulge in the fun, noise and excitement of the fair. Annie Wilson would be taken by her father. 'There was a brass band on the front and there was either a couple of monkeys or a bear or something all chained up. Oh you used to stand fascinated. . . . And then he'd take us to the stall. For very few coppers he bought us all one of those little sticks of brandy snap.' There were coconut shies and side shows, hoop-las, swings, hurdy-gurdies and waxworks. Toy stalls sold penny toys and a satisfied child would leave with an acrobat on a wire, or a wooden figure that raised his hat, a piece of miniature dolls' furniture or a Chinese tumbler that rolled over and over. Donkey races

amused the crowds, while boxing fights drew cheers and encouraging shouts.

Village fairs and fêtes generally involved the entire population of the area in morris dancing and pageants, competitions and sports. The children had a wonderful time eating toffee apples or sticky gingerbreads while waiting for their turn on the swings and roundabouts. Rachel Ferguson recalls a local fête that '. . . carried on until night, when the grounds were illuminated and when one reads of the attractions it's a wonder that midnight saw it through. For besides many side shows there was a croquet tournament, a rose show, a cake competition, a fancy dress cricket match and a limerick competition judged by Sir W.S. Gilbert. There were . . . a Dutch auction, supper, and finally a concert party, "The Charivari White Coons". The prices were staggering. Sixpence for a motor-launch trip up and down the river, sixpence for a plate of strawberries and cream; tea, of bread and butter and cakes, sixpence, supper two shillings . . ..'

Electric Palaces

Many of the fairgrounds of the early twentieth century were changing from side shows to moving picture shows. The fairgrounds had used small booth theatres for the presentation of clowns and acrobats, and the stage was now adapted for showing films. The fashion had started with an amusement machine that Cynthia Asquith first came across at Earls Court. 'There we first enjoyed

A street fair offered exciting market stalls as well as amusements.

cinema entranced the young viewers. They would save their pennies so that they could join the agitated and excited queue, buy their tickets for threepence and spend a couple of hours inside that magic house. Some parents disapproved and called the cinemas 'fleapits' and 'bug hutches', but others thought them safer than theatres, as Florence Atherton recalls: 'We went to the cinema occasionally, but mother would never let us go to a theatre or music hall. She was always afraid of a fire, always dreaded a fire.'

By 1914, many of the music halls had been converted to cinemas to meet the demand for more moving picture shows, and were given such names as Bijou, Gem, Pallasino and Picturedrome.

the germ of the cinematograph – penny-in-the-slot machine in which, by turning a handle, you saw simple and sometimes "risky" stories told by photographs.'

In towns the first 'electric palaces' were built and attracted hordes of children on Saturday afternoons for thrilling shows of Western battles between cowboys and Indians, adventure stories and Charlie Chaplin comedies. Arthur Newton realized that 'Entertainment was altering too. The new-fangled "Moving Picture Theatre" was creeping up on us. People up to now had relied on the Music Hall and their own family gatherings to pass an evening away, but now were able to see real moving pictures. No sound – not yet – that was to come around 1928.' Those early films were not designed for juvenile audiences, but the flickering shadows and the fantasy world of the

Suspension of Disbelief

Wealthy Edwardian children were taken to plays and concerts at a very young age, usually to matinees, but sometimes to evening performances. Ruby Ferguson remembers an afternoon treat: 'At two o'clock we were at Queen's Hall to see the greatest magic show of all time, two hours of mystifying, polished illusion . . . and one of the finest entertainments in London.' The theatre played an important part in the life of Diana Cooper's family: 'Since the age of two when I was taken to see Marie Tempest in *The Geisha* we went a lot to the theatre. . . . My mother's love of the beautiful in everything took us to Her Majesty's Theatre for every production and repeatedly to all Shakespeare's plays. We were a family brought up on both sides of the Beerbohm Trees' velvet curtain. . . . Musical comedies were allowed, if unvulgar. I remember being too young for *The Belle of New York*, though I could sing 'Follow On' . . .. I liked the thrill of night better than a matinée and so we went in the evenings. It meant at extra sleep from tea to 7.30 and sometimes (before Henry V, I remember) being sick from excitement.'

Cynthia Asquith was equally spellbound by the theatre: '. . . the real glory of the London of my early memories is of course as the place in which I first knew those pinnacles of all childhood experiences, FIRST THEATRES. . . . I was nine when I was taken to my first play, *The Two Little Vagabonds*, a curdling melodrama in which even the hero, an undersized and wholly innocent child of exactly my own age, was stabbed to death. On my return almost unconscious from the theatre, I was catastrophically sick in the hall and so ill afterwards from overexcitement than I had to stay in bed for a fortnight.'

Theatres offered a wide selection of serious drama, musical comedy, light opera, melodramas, ballet, concerts and pantomimes. David Garnett tells how 'An early visit to London to the dentist was followed by a visit to my aunt and uncle . . .. In the evening I was taken to a pantomime. The comic man had a bald head, with a central tuft of hair rising up like a cock's comb, and his loud voice, vulgarity and easy familiar manner terrified and disgusted me.' But Gervas Huxley was more impressed: 'The greatest treat of the whole year was The Drury Lane Pantomime. . . . We went, of course, to the matinee and sat in the Dress Circle. . . . The Drury Lane Panto was then in the heyday of its glory, with Dan Leno and Herbert Campbell as its star comedians. The show lasted a good four hours, so we got full measure.' Ellen Terry, Adeline Genée, Isadora Duncan, Enrico Caruso, Maud Allan, George Robey, Vesta Tilley, Adelina Patti and Madame Melba all appeared regularly at the favourite theatres. Even poor children managed to find a way of seeing the shows, and Anna Blair, writing of her life in Glasgow in 1902, recalls: 'They used to show plays on Saturday afternoons . . . you could get in for nothin' and a free programme half-way through, and pester your neighbour to tell you what happened in the first half.' Like many others, Stephen Potter thought theatre far superior to cinema, writing: 'Any comparison between the theatre and cinema . . . would then have been to the overwhelming disadvantage of the latter . . ..'

Other Urban Treats

In the streets there were barrel organs whose music urged the children to dance, and Jack London wrote: 'There is one beautiful sight in the East End, and one only, and it is the children dancing in the street when the organ grinder goes his round. It is fascinating to watch them, the new born, the next generation, swaying and stepping . . . weaving rhythms never taught in dancing

Sundays were also days of local entertainments for those who took a stroll through nearby parks and gardens. Bands often performed on bandstands between 11 a.m. and 1 p.m. from March to October and sometimes, very bravely, during the winter months, too. Children scampered on the grass or whipped tops and trundled hoops, while parents showed off their best clothes and chatted with neighbours or just stood listening to the music.

On Sunday evenings concerts were held in local halls and theatres, often organized by the National Sunday League. Little children were told to be careful not to muddy or dirty their clothes as they walked along the road to the concert halls like little dolls beside their parents.

Punch and Judy's antics and shrieks always drew a crowd.

school.' Punch and Judy shows also drew little crowds of laughing children. Diana Cooper remembered seeing '. . . very rarely the dramas of Punch's life and Judy's death and Toby's indifference ringed round with a knot of smaller children, cabbies, and flocks of pigeons and sparrows squabbling for the grain that fell from the poor horse's nosebag.'

Street vendors and pedlars arrived with other small treats. All through the week there were the men with trays of winkles and shrimps, watercress and baked potatoes. A favourite was the ice-cream man selling a questionable mixture of crushed, sweetened ice, egg and milk made into a creamy slush that to the children was delicious. Then on winter Sundays came the muffin man and children pressed their noses to the window to see the great tray carried on the man's head, and wait hopefully for their mother to send them out with a few pennies to buy some for tea.

Out for the Day
Many families enjoyed trips together on their bicycles, and a picnic at the end of the ride was really something to look forward to. Improvements and advances in public transport meant that all but the very poor could afford a ride on a tram, train, tube or bus and go to visit friends or relatives in another part of the town, or go off into the country for the day. Rich families often had their own motor car, and sat in comfort while the family chauffeur drove through country lanes and along new highways. The appeal of the early cars was not the comfort but the speed, the new technology and the independence that they gave. A day out in a motor car was seen as a real

adventure, since neither driver nor passengers really knew if the vehicle would arrive at its destination. The engine might cut out at any moment, tyres might get stuck in the mud or slide dangerously on patches of ice or water, or the car might bump into another motor coming in the opposite direction along a narrow, windy road. Even the drivers themselves did not always inspire much confidence. Madge Hodson tells of the occasion that her family went off in the new car to visit relatives. As the car swept into the driveway of the relatives' house, the chauffeur did not seem quite sure how to control the powerful machine and it careered forward and banged into the steps leading up to the front door, sending the waiting family scurrying inside in terror.

Out on the roads, visibility was poor, road surfaces were rough, corners and junctions were hazardous, and petrol supplies were few and far between. To cyclists, horses and pedestrians, the motor car was a filthy, noisy, smelly, frightening machine, but to the owner it was enormous fun. Ruby Ferguson recalls one incident in the country: 'We bobbed low as the machine, an uncommon sight in the country lanes, went past. It made an awful din, but the men and women sitting high seemed to be enjoying themselves. They wore dust coats and goggles, and as they passed the man gave

May Day was a special time in rural communities and every village had its maypole and flower garlands.

131

a warning toot on his horn and the alien noise sent a chitter of starlings up above the hedge.'

For those who could not afford their own car and had to rely on public transport, trams, trains and horsedrawn omnibuses provided an excellent service, with plenty of double- and single-decker trams and buses running long distances around suburban areas and to nearby town and villages. In London, so many companies plied for customers that at the beginning of the century, on an average day, six hundred and ninety omnibuses an hour were reported to have passed the Bank and six hundred and twenty two through Piccadilly Circus. The electrification of the railways led to cheaper and faster trains, and with the choice of all these modern means of transport, parents and children could easily travel out into the countryside for half a day and leave the dirt and noise of the town far behind.

Countryside Treats

For children living in rural areas, a farming life provided its own special occasions. At harvest all the family became labourers to bind the sheaves and pile them in stooks, and the fun came at lunch time when baskets laden with sandwiches, bread, cheese, cakes and pies arrived from the farmhouse with some of the women. When the children had finished eating, they played hide and seek among the stooks until it was time to start work again. Mary Wright describes how mealtimes were shared by all: 'Women and children walked out from the house sometimes along lanes and over fields, carrying a large basket and a pitcher or kettle of hot tea.... The basket was lined with white cloths: one half contained all the cups and the other half was filled with freshly baked food.... Everybody sat down in the field and ate together, and this was as great a treat for the children as for the workers. There would be no crumbs left to carry back.'

The beginning of May was another festive treat for village children and, in some cases, for town dwellers. Flora Thompson's memory is that 'For the children as the day approached all hardships were forgotten and troubles melted away. The only thing that mattered was the weather. "Will it be fine?" was the constant question.' She goes on to explain that early on May morning 'All the children in the parish between the ages of 7 and 11 were by this time assembled, those girls who possessed them wearing white or light-coloured frocks, irrespective of the temperature, and the girls and boys alike decked out with bright ribbon knots and bows and sashes....' Walter Greenwood tells how 'This was our time, we who were young ... not a street, however mean, that did not have its group of little girls preparing for the first of May. Each street, when the day dawned, had its maypole, a broom handle festooned with coloured tissues and hanging with multi-coloured ribbons.... A ring of girls, each holding a ribbon in attendance on a diminuitive May Queen veiled with a piece of old lace curtain and carrying a basket of posies and a collecting tin for the hoped-for half-penny contributions' then set off to sing and dance at every door in the village.

Sunday School Treats

The best treat of all for many children was the annual Sunday School outing. These tea treats originated with the religious processions around villages and towns that were organized by various church groups and that were always followed by hymn singing and a huge tea. The event gradually became a festival for the children, and the parish would arrange a trip to a nearby beauty spot or place of interest, as Mary Wright describes: 'Their teachers rode on farm waggons horse- or later tractor-drawn, which had been carefully cleaned for the occasion and decorated with greenery and bunting. Older children and adults followed on, "walking their legs off".' Arthur Newton remembers: 'Many a good day I have had to Theydon Bois in Epping Forest by horse brake. It was a good journey in those days. No fast motor cars, the horses jogged along, the kids were singing, streamers and paper windmills were in plenty. Who couldn't afford a half-penny streamer with about 4d in one's pocket? Usually collected from auntie or mum or grown up sister Sue. . . . Must buy a present for Mum! A penny vase, a cheap necklace, or lavender in a bag from a gypsy.'

The children had a wonderful time and a free tea. Leonard Clark recalls: 'We would eat bread and butter as if our lives depended on it, and drink gallons of sweet tea as if destined for the remainder of the day to be turned loose in the Sahara. The cakes would disappear faster than they could be replenished by our teachers, and we would fill in the moments waiting by returning the attack on the bread and butter.' In Cornwall, special saffron-flavoured buns were distributed, and when the food was gone there were games and sports. Leonard Clark goes on: 'While the grown-ups were having their tea, we were free to wander about the field. We would venture on the swings or on a large see-saw set up specially for the occasion, or walk about with our friends. Sooner or later, however, we would all be wandering round the stalls and spending our store of pennies on bull's-eyes, acid drops, monkey nuts and tiger nuts, locust beans and aniseed balls.' Then there were flat races, three-legged races, book-on-the-head races, egg-and-spoon races, obstacle races and lots of prizes (usually second-hand caps, ties, pencils, paint-boxes and such like).

It is perhaps difficult today to understand why Edwardian children found shopping exciting, or how the unsteady flickering pictures of the early cinema or a ride in a cab inspired such interest and wonder. But for all Edwardian children, both rich and poor, the days were punctuated by these special events and new experiences. A rigid routine and strict discipline meant that the lighter moments of life, no matter how trivial, were regarded as treats, and were looked forward to and remembered with joy and gratitude.

HIGH DAYS AND HOLIDAYS

For all Edwardian children, the idea of a whole day spent away from home and school was very exciting, and holidays were an almost indescribably wonderful luxury. Journeys by steam train or electric tram were still an adventure and gave a sense of travelling away into the unknown. Even a journey by horsedrawn carriage that took passengers from a small rural village to a nearby town was a rare treat and provided an opportunity for the intrepid young traveller to see how others lived and what magical items were on offer in the big town shops. Leonard Clark could hardly wait for the day to come when he and his mother were to travel fourteen miles from their village to Gloucester: 'The journey took three hours there and four hours back, three hours downhill in the light, and four hours uphill in the dark. It was made by horse-brake, and I can see that vehicle now in my mind's eye, as clear and brightly painted as on the day when it first set out. . . . The day of days would come at last – Mother and I would get up at six-thirty, there would be much polishing of boots, brushing down of clothes, packing of sandwiches, counting of pennies. . . . There I would be, with my well-scrubbed shining face, carefully ironed white lace collar, Norfolk breeches and squeaking boots.'

Wide Open Spaces

The great joy of cheap modern transport was that it made travel accessible to all but the very poor, and families could escape from the densely-populated towns to enjoy the fresh air, the green fields, the woods and open spaces of the surrounding countryside, or the salt air and seaside smells of the nearby coastal resorts. A.L. Rowse writes that when he and his friends knew that they were going off to the sea for the day, '. . . we couldn't have been more excited and tingling with expectancy if we were making a journey into Darkest Africa. . . . We paddled; hardly anybody bathed in those days: we ran about the Winnick [grass covered dunes], played games and quarrelled. . . .' The railway companies offered special Sunday excursions in conjunction with the National Sunday League. 2/6d bought seven hours at the seaside, and passengers would arrive at the chosen resort at 2 o'clock in the afternoon and depart again at 9 o'clock in the evening.

The seaside was probably more alluring than

The golden sand and the sparkling sea were a source of pure delight.

Cheap fares on the railways allowed families to enjoy a day out at the sea or in the country.

the countryside, with its seaweed smells, sea breezes, sand that trickled through your toes and all the entertainments on the promenade or the pier. But, if the sea was too far away, then a day in the country was the next best thing. Some families left the town for the day just to explore new ground and have a break from the noise and dirt of the city. Others joined cycling clubs and set off to see how far they could travel in one day. Parents and children went to seek new species of wild flowers, and youngsters brought their discoveries home and carefully pressed and mounted them in special albums. Rambling clubs became very popular and campaigns were organized to maintain public footpaths and protect areas of forest and common land. Families of hikers set out together with maps and compasses to explore new territory, and anglers of all ages headed for streams and rivers, or seaside piers.

Movable Feasts

In these early days of trips to the sea and the country, the picnic became a popular and indeed essential pleasure, for it was not easy to find refreshments. Wayside inns, pubs and tea-rooms provided lunches and teas, but once you were off the main highways, the only way to feed the family was by transporting a picnic meal. Hampers were packed with cold meats and pies, potted fish, cheeses, bread, favourite sandwiches, cakes, fruit pies and biscuits. Home-made lemonade and ginger beer satisfied the children's thirst, and the

newly-invented thermos flask carried hot soups and drinks for the grown-ups. A little spirit primus stove was already a favourite piece of picnic equipment, and as soon as a suitable spot had been chosen, the kettle was set to boil while children climbed trees, flew kites and chased each other across open fields and moors.

Sonia Keppel enjoyed picnics on many occasions. While staying in Scotland, 'The high spots of our stay were our picnics on the banks of Loch Lomond. Beside it, happily we unpacked our baskets while the water lapped gently at our feet and the stillness gradually enveloped us.' Since her parents were great friends of the King, they were

Holiday pennies were spent on refreshing treats.

often among his party when elaborate day excursions were planned. The food was always wonderful, but the spot chosen not quite so alluring: 'Every variety of cold food was produced, spiced by iced cup in silver-plated containers. For some unfathomed reason, Kingy had a preference for picnicking by the side of the road. On Easter Day, inevitably, this was packed with carriages and the first motor-cars, all covered with dust, and when we parked by the roadside most of the traffic parked with us.'

Country picnics for poorer people involved more modest food and drink than that of the royal party, but were just as much fun for those taking part. David Marriot remembers how, in 1909, 'We'd picnic down Jack's orchard. You'd get your big jug of skim milk to go wi' your piece'n'jam and teeter away down the field tryin' not to slop it afore you got sat down under a special big apple-tree.'

Beside the Seaside

Some lucky children were able to enjoy the sea not just for an odd day here and there, but for a month or so every year when the family group, made up of Mother and possibly her sisters or sisters-in-law, their respective nannies and various children, migrated from town villa, terraced house or country mansion to a favourite resort beside the sea. Fathers usually stayed behind to continue working, but often joined the family at weekends. Stephen Potter writes: 'The edge of our appetite for the sea was never taken off by casual day-trips to the south coast. The act of booking seats in a train and emerging into the New Place made the experience more complete.'

It was the era of fresh air and exercise, and the seaside was considered the ideal environment for young and old to recoup from the daily toil of life in the towns. Those with relatives who lived near the sea could descend on aunts and grandparents for their annual holiday. Others rented houses or

Shoes and socks came off and spades were put to work to build the biggest castle.

rooms, or put up at hotels. Henry Vigne writes: 'When we were small we used to go to Felixstowe . . . I think we used to go every year until I was about eight or nine. Father and Mother used to . . . stay in a hotel and we used to stay in a boarding house. The two elder girls stayed in the hotel with Father and Mother, and the three young ones stayed in the boarding house. I think we used to

families often stayed in expensive hotels or high-class lodging houses. The less well-off were happy with lodgings where the landlady cooked all the meals with food bought by each mother. In rented houses and cottages, a resident cook or house-keeper often shopped and cooked for the family.

Diana Cooper tells how her 'idyllic life was varied by visits to Belvoir (her grandfather's castle

During Cowes week, there was always something to watch from the promenade.

stay in a lodging house which was kept by a relative of our nurse. . . .' Some parents liked the hubbub and excitement of the busy, established resorts such as Blackpool, Southend, Eastbourne or Brighton, where there were tennis courts, golf courses, race tracks and entertainments. Others preferred quieter towns such as Frinton, Lowes-toft or Clevedon. For those who did not like to be near a town at all, an isolated cottage or a country house near a quiet beach was an ideal spot. Smart

in Leicestershire) and to Sussex, where my mother rented cottages beside the summer sea. . . . Sussex by the sea was wonderfully different. . . . I never went there until I was six, and I was disappointed by the beach. It was middle tide when I first saw the sea, with rows and rows of little long white waves. I had imagined something generally bigger with occasional breakers the size of hills, but the sand was a delight that I had not been told to expect.' Her family once stayed in a '. . . four-roomed thatched cottage called Priors Farm, from which we walked through acres of waving corn to the tamarisk hedge that protected it from the sea. A tired old dear cooked and cleaned and heated water for washing.'

Gervas Huxley was sent off to the sea with his sister: 'Each year, soon after Christmas, Marjorie and I were packed off to Eastbourne in the charge of our nurse in order to benefit from the sea air. We were well wrapped up for the train journey from Victoria Station, since, on the Eastbourne line, the non-corridor compartments had no form of heating other than iron footwarmers filled with hot water which, on request, a porter would place in the carriage.'

For families that could not afford to take their children to the seaside every summer, charitable bodies such as The Children's Country Holiday Fund and the Pearson Fresh Air Fund organized holidays and day trips for the youngsters.

Getting There

The preparation for the annual holiday occupied Nanny and Mother for several weeks before the appointed departure date.

Jocelyn Brooke remembers all the preparations in fine detail: '... the real journey – the train journey, that is to say – began from Shorncliffe; but hardly less exciting were the preparatory phases of the great expedition: the ... bustle of departure, the unfamiliar aspect of rooms covered in dust sheets or (if the house were to be let for the

summer) with their more valuable ornaments removed and the furniture rearranged.' Sonia Keppel's family went off on fashionable trips abroad, and 'It took Nannie weeks to prepare for our Easter holiday in Biarritz, as the whole of Violet's and my wardrobe had to be checked over and brought up to date.'

Boxes and trunks had to be packed with enormous supplies of clothes and hats for all occasions and weather conditions, and supplies of buckets and spades, toys and games were essential for the children. Some families even took their tin bath with them so that the children could be well scrubbed after their frolics on the beach. When everything was ready, it was loaded into the family car or transported to the railway station by a horsedrawn carriage that was provided by the railway company or hired out specially for the event. The men who were employed to carry and load all the luggage on to the roof then ran alongside all the way to the station, hoping for a generous tip when the work was done and the baggage and passengers were safely stowed in the train. The journey was complicated and cumbersome, but all the packing, loading and transporting added to the sense of adventure and excitement. Jocelyn Brooke tells how 'Ninnie and I would set forth, at last, in a cab upon the preliminary trek to the frontier-station of Shorncliffe.... At a later date we would sometimes make the whole journey by car; but at this period our annual migrations followed an invariable routine: Ninnie and I – a kind of advance party – would travel by train (taking with us, incidentally, the greater part of the luggage) while the rest of the family followed in the motor. (It was called the "motor" in those days – an old-fashioned Singer, with a high driver's seat, a cumbrous and unmanageable hood, and enormous brass head-lamps.)'

Sonia Keppel travelled to Scotland by train. 'At Carlisle, we were allowed out of the train for ten precarious minutes, dogged by my fear that the train might proceed without us. During this time we were allowed a change of magazine, and bottled sweets, at the bookstall. And here too, we took our luncheon basket . . . mammoth rolls of bread containing sides of chicken. The meal tasted

Dressed in such bizarre outfits, early motorists were often figures of fun.

delicious, consisting of the otherwise forbidden fruits of cheddar cheese and unripe pears. And there was the fun of putting out the basket at the next station.'

As the journey reached its end, there was always great excitement and anticipation, described here by Sybil Pearce: 'We arrived at the house in a horse-drawn brougham from Fareham, and the loud crunch of the golden gravelled roads under the wooden wheels of the carriage was one of my first thrills. I felt that we were alone in the country lane and that our carriage was making the only sound in the world.'

Sand and Sea

Once at the seaside, the sand and sea were the main attractions but many children were not allowed to swim or even paddle during the first few days. Joan Poynder '. . . dug in the sand. I don't remember doing anything else very much but going down to the beach and paddling. . . . You were never allowed to paddle or bathe till you'd been there about a couple of days. . . . We dug with a wooden spade or something, one always wanted to buy the iron ones . . . and one always got a new bucket, a shrimping net and a boat, and you paddled and bathed.' Diana Cooper also loved playing on the beach: 'Nanny and we children undressed for bathing in a little coppice at the end of the garden. There would be murmurs of "turn your back" and lo! Nanny was dressed in bloomers and tunic of shocking pink. . . . There was never a

The new electric underground trains allowed cheap and easy travel across London.

question of learning to swim, but we splashed in the waves or crab-dabbled wearing waders and picking up cuttle-fish or decorating our sand-castles with tamarisk.... In my earliest days at Bognor I remember being in a bathing-machine drawn into four feet of water by a carthorse, and dipped head and all into the sea by the old bathing-woman, her long skirt billowing in the water.' Sea baths were thought to be good for children, but many parents would not allow any child under the age of eight or so to go into the sea because it was thought highly dangerous. However, in some resorts, swimming lessons were offered so that the youngsters could enjoy the waves and still remain safe. Along the beaches were a few outmoded bathing machines, but the more fashionable beaches now had canvas tents and wooden huts where holiday-makers could change and store their beach paraphernalia. Japanese parasols also became very popular and the sands were dotted with these colourful sunshades.

During Edwardian years an increased liberalism allowed ladies to bathe direct from the beach instead of being pulled into the waves in one of the old machines. Mixed bathing was allowed in Bexhill-on-Sea as early as 1901, and swimsuits were accepted as normal beach attire. But at other resorts, bathing remained segregated until 1914, and cloaks were provided for female bathers to wear as they walked to and from the water's edge.

At the turn of the century, little boys and girls were expected to wear all their normal clothes on the beach. Smart navy sailor suits and straw or felt hats or caps were the usual garb, but it was permitted to pull off shoes and socks or stockings when it was time for a paddle in the sea. Sybil Pearce remembers that at Hill Head in Hampshire 'I now wore a sailor suit with a blue serge kilt and a big straw hat and went cockling on the sands and prawning with the grown-ups who went out daily to bring back prawns for tea.' Later in the decade, boys were more often seen in shorts and jerseys, while little girls still wore dresses or pinafores. Children's bathing suits were made of alpaca, serge, flannel or corduroy and had knee-length bloomers and skirts to the thigh for the girls. Although they were uncomfortable, the children were at least a little freer in these than in their day clothes. As the years passed, so the comfort and practicality of swimwear improved and children were soon running around in two-tone cotton or jersey swimsuits with thigh-length legs. But babies were kept well wrapped in several layers of frills and lace, coverlets and capes.

John Betjeman loved every moment of his days at the seaside:

Then before breakfast down toward the sea
I ran alone, monarch of miles of sand,
Its shining stretches satin-smooth and vein'd.
Wet rocks on which our bathing dresses dried;
Small coves, deserted in our later years
For more adventurous inlets down the coast.

Brightly striped tents replaced Victorian bathing machines and provided shade from the midday sun.

Holiday Treats

During holidays, parents and nannies tended to relax their codes of discipline and allowed the children special treats – an hour extra before having to go to bed; special teas in sea-front tea-rooms or elegant palm court restaurants in posh hotels; ice creams and sweets from booths on the pier; picnics on the sand; family photographs taken by professionals on the beach, visits to Punch and Judy shows on the beach or concerts and variety shows in the winter gardens or theatres.

Seaside towns overflowed with entertainments for adults and children. If there was a pier, it was the main attraction and offered all sorts of fun, from fairground rides on swings and helter-

skelters to roller-skating rinks, stalls and barrows selling cockles and winkles, booths that sheltered fortune-tellers, souvenir shops crammed with shells and sand-filled objects, pencil cases, ashtrays, mugs, boxes, porcelain pots and postcards.

Children saved their pennies to buy little mementoes for Nanny or for Father, who had remained behind in the city. Sebastian's nanny in *Brideshead Revisited* has a mantelpiece in the nursery decorated with '... the collection of small presents which had been brought home to her at various times by her children, carved shell and lava, stamped leather, painted wood, china, bog-oak, damascened silver, blue-john, alabaster, coral, the souvenirs of many holidays.'

There were any number of things on which to spend pocket money. Fairgrounds tempted with big wheels, merry-go-rounds and target-shooting games. Shops were crammed with brightly-coloured buckets and spades and little wooden wheelbarrows for moving sand around on the beach. Rows of shrimping nets stood propped against shop windows and walls, and sticks of rock just begged to be purchased from counters that dazzled customers with their array of coloured sweets, cheap jewellery and toys. Rows of slot machines offered, for a penny, almanacks, perfume, matches, razor blades, sweets, cigarettes and drinks. Some really up-to-date machines would even tell your weight or take your photograph. Magic lanterns and mutoscopes showed sequences

of photographs that were mounted on a drum and made a short motion picture when a handle was cranked. The public's appetite for entertainment and amusement became more and more demanding and each summer some new invention had children running to indulgent parents to plead for another penny to push into the slot. Rachel Ferguson recalls one such distraction: 'In a side

Donkeys waited patiently on the sand to give rides to small children.

turning near the hotel was a shooting gallery and sweet shop . . .. Here, for a half-penny a shot, we aimed at ping-pong balls tossing on a water jet and at a ballet-girl target.' On the beach, groups of donkeys stood patiently waiting to take little tots for a gentle ride along the sand. There were rowing boats for hire and advertisements for trips on steamers and paddle boats. Groups of children would cluster round the port or harbour to watch the boats to-ing and fro-ing and to see the fishing fleet come in with their decks squirming and wriggling with the fresh catch.

On the beach and promenade, singers, dance troupes and musicians entertained the crowds in canvas tents or bandstands. The German bands and minstrel shows of the late nineteenth century were replaced by the more fashionable pierrot groups, who, dressed in baggy suits with black pom-poms, provided family entertainment that was of a much higher standard than the more commonly seen street buskers. Their rivals, the fol-de-rols or follies, sang and played in similar shows; and concert parties, in nautical outfits or smart suits and panama hats, performed songs, music and variety acts. Some of these groups also played in the elegant restaurants and tea-rooms, so that dancing couples could display their skills at the tango and the foxtrot. Tea-rooms were far more popular than their rivals, the itinerant salesmen. On very hot days families sought shelter from the glaring sun, and quenched their thirst with pots of tea and ice creams; and on cold, wet and windy days they sheltered from unkind weather and comforted themselves with platefuls of cream cakes and sticky buns.

Bother the Rain

If the sun did not shine, and the rain came to spoil their holiday fun, the children had to resort to indoor games to occupy themselves until the weather improved. Well-organized families came prepared with a supply of favourite toys and board games, jigsaws, cards and miniature indoor versions of outdoor games. Fingers flicked the small ball of an indoor cricket match across the floor, and carpet bowls, rather like large marbles, were rolled skilfully in the same way as outdoor bowls. Indoor croquet, with miniature hoops, mallets and balls, was played either on the floor or on a cloth-covered table-top; and ninepins, an adapted version of skittles, was another favourite. Quoits and tiddly-winks were ideal indoor amusements, and, if there was a table and a room big enough, the newly-invented ping-pong, or table tennis, kept children happy for hours. Parents were often tempted to join in all these challenging games, and pouring rain and high winds would often be forgotten in the fun and laughter of the parlour or playroom.

Travels Abroad

Some wealthy parents took their families right away from Britain's unpredictable weather and holidayed in the sun of the fashionable French resorts and Italian beauty spots. Or they boarded elegant liners and cruised the Caribbean or the Mediterranean. For such trips, servants and parents made sure that medicine chests and first aid kits were included in the baggage, just in case any of the children succumbed to some foreign disease. Along with shoe boxes, hat boxes, wardrobe trunks and jewel cases, there were travelling rugs and cushions for comfort on the journey, and bags of books and toys to amuse the younger members of the party. Gervas Huxley writes: 'It was, of course, a tremendous excitement to cross the Channel, to see French gendarmes at Calais Pier and to hear a foreign language spoken.'

Here Diana Cooper describes setting out on her first trip to Florence: 'My father, unsympathetic to travel, gave her [Diana's mother] a hundred pounds to cover tickets and all expenses. . . . Our luggage and paraphernalia was prodigious. Little was trusted abroad, so everything must be taken from home – a pharmacopoeia, a clinical thermometer (French ones being unusable) with spares in case of breakage, umbrellas rolled in rugs, sunshades of natural-coloured cotton lined with dark blue or green. . . . Guards and porters from London to Dover were questioned about the state of the sea. My mother took an opium pill but I, on a steamer for the first time, was determined to feel like a figurehead.'

Sonia Keppel and her family stayed at the Villa Eugénie in Biarritz, where: 'No doubt designed for

the Prince Imperial, the nurseries were ornate and formal and, like the rest of the villa, seemed always prepared for an invisible party. . . . Uneasily, Nannie, Violet and I settled into them.'

But these adventurous holidays in foreign places were only for the rich, and most children were happy to romp on British beaches. As the decade progressed, British resorts became more and more popular, each one developing its own particular qualities and attracting certain types of holiday-makers with pubs, dance halls, concert halls, amusement arcades, souvenir shops, golf courses, sight-seeing tours, restaurants and tea-rooms. *Punch* wrote of one of the south coast's busiest resorts: 'Saturday and Monday, and every working day in a summer week, Bournemouth is blithe and gay. Steamers are running hither and thither, wagonettes, coaches, gardens with music, excellent bands on a well-appointed pier, concerts, donkey-riding, al fresco refreshments, clowns – in fact everything that is considered by the majority as constituting a 'appy 'oliday, is to be found, at its best, at Bournemouth.' Who needed France or Italy? Who needed expensive trips to funny foreign parts? No! British beaches were good enough for the hoards of people that flocked there every summer. They were not worried by bad weather – what they wanted was the fresh air, the smell of the sea, the sand to play on, a little freedom from the grime and noise of the city and a chance to enjoy being beside the sea.

CAUSE FOR CELEBRATION

Edwardian children celebrated their birthdays in much the same way as children today, with presents and cards and cakes and parties. Of course children from wealthy families were spoilt with expensive gifts, visits to the theatre or the zoo and elaborate cakes, whereas poorer children often had to make do with very small presents and no festivities. In Clifford Hills's family, for example, 'There was no particular celebration for birthdays. There wasn't too much money to celebrate, only Christmas.' But for Jack Yorke it was different: 'We looked forward to birthdays. They were quite an occasion. . . . We used to have a children's party . . . and we generally had a children's party in the Christmas time. . . .' Joan Poynder recalls: 'On my birthday I had all the usual things, a party and a cake. Mother and Father's friends' children came. My mother played Blind Man's Buff. But I don't remember her playing the other games. Old Maid and things like that. . . . There were fancy dress parties . . . and dancing and cotillions and mostly dancing with music. . . .' Cynthia Asquith's fifth birthday was celebrated in great style. 'The magnolia on the

A fancy dress party was a wonderful way to celebrate a birthday.

Birthday parties usually included a cake and the traditional blowing out of the candles.

sugar coated cake, the glimmer of the five green candles and the horrid smell when they were blown out; my unavowed dread of crackers, the tickling glory of the "Birthday Girl's" crown – for the occasion my mother always made us wreaths of flowers – and some mighty grown-up hand guiding my own to cut the cake. "All for me!" I remember thinking.'

Rachel Ferguson also enjoyed beautifully decorated cakes: 'Birthday teas were memorable, for not only were table and sideboard massed with cakes, but fat, gleaming crackers were piled about, and centring all was the cake itself. Every October it was a different design. One was a witch's cave, its rocks of iced cake and the witch surrounded by net money-bags filled with chocolate sovereigns: another was a may-pole made of a ribbon-bound sugar-stick, and circling the cake were little plaster dancers in pastel shades, each holding a ribbon. When tea was over, every guest received one.... How good those parties smelt! With no wireless and cine-cameras, mothers had to be inventive, and I think we had more fun at infinitely less outlay than is possible now.' Rachel goes on to describe many different types of party. 'I remember a real miniature dinner-party (at night! Seven to nine).... It was held in the nursery and we sat round a small table and the son of the house carved a tiny roast bird.... At another party, an iced cake was by every place with the name of the guest inscribed on it in pink sugar.... There was the party with the facetious conjurer who, then as

now, was of an absolute competence.' She also explains that nurses or nannies, '... were their nursling old enough ... were even able to share in the birthday teas in the dining-room and get a sight of conjurer, magic lantern or ventriloquist in the drawing-room.

Easter Festivities

As the year progressed, there were plenty of excuses to celebrate. For children from wealthy families Easter meant chocolate eggs and parties and special meals, while for poorer families it just meant a time of special church services and perhaps a joint of roast veal or lamb for Sunday lunch. In many parts of the country, particularly near the coast. Easter celebrations started on Good Friday, when family groups headed for rivers and beaches in search of fresh fish and shellfish. Mary Wright describes how in West Cornwall '... Good Friday was the traditional day for "trigging". Whole families trekked from the Lizard peninsular to the Helford River, and from the Camborne-Redruth area to Godrevy and North Cliffs to gather "trig-meat" [shellfish]. Armed with sticks and rakes, buckets and bags, hundreds of people dug for thousands of cockles and any other shellfish they could find. Many diggers built fires on the beach and boiled the fish in water; many more preferred to do it at home.'

For middle- and upper-class families the festivities were more sophisticated. Cynthia Asquith spent Easter at her grandparents' house. 'We always went to Clouds for Easter – a festival kept by Gan Gan with as much ceremony – hundreds of eggs hidden all over the garden and the house – as Christmas.' Sonia Keppel travelled abroad with her parents and the King's social circle for the festive weekend. 'Easter Sunday at Biarritz was an occasion for giving beautiful presents. And not only the grown-ups. Still I have lovely little jewelled Easter eggs given me by Kingy, particularly an exquisitely midget one in royal blue enamel, embossed with a diamond 'E', and topped by a tiny crown in gold and rubies. Beach parties and parties with other children took up our time and on Easter Sunday, Kingy, ourselves and a host of others set forth for a mammoth picnic.'

The Fifth of November

Bonfire Night on 5 November was another annual event for some children. Rachel Ferguson's family spent time building a memorable bonfire with the help of the gardener. 'Our gardener "Old James" (he was probably forty odd) got £1 a half-day week except on the Fifth of November when he came round to oversee the bonfire and help let off the fireworks. . . . Of all the parties that Mother gave, our Fifth of November celebrations ranked high. With ample kitchen garden space we fairly let ourselves go. One year, we had a tableau of Kruger in the grip of a life-sized red devil. When the flames burnt the strings, Kruger dropped into the fire. Another guy was a current woman murderess. . . .'

An Edwardian Christmas

Edwardian Christmases involved several new customs that had only recently become part of the British celebrations. The Victorians had introduced the idea of the Christmas tree, but the Edwardians developed further the custom of hanging presents as well as tinsel and colourful decorations on its branches. The giving of cards was also a relatively new fashion, and the choice of cards with suitable pictures and greetings involved as much care as the selection of presents. The idea of exchanging gifts became an essential part of the modern Christmas, although some people still preferred the old custom of offering gifts on New Year's Day instead of Christmas Day. Advertisements started to appear in shops, newspapers and magazines to encourage people to choose something suitable for children and relatives. In 1898 *The Times* carried advertisements suggesting blankets, dress-lengths, musical boxes, jewellery, oil paintings, sweets, oysters at 48/- a barrel of sixteen dozen, encyclopedias, diaries and books. Bazaars and exhibitions offered cards and hand-made gifts, and shops displayed such objects as Christmas annuals, indoor games and hampers specially produced for the seasonal market.

The Christmas Tree

Prince Albert had played a major part in popularizing the idea of the Christmas tree when he set one up at Windsor Castle in 1840. Wealthy families copied the royal example, and by the late nineteenth century thousands of trees were bought every year and set up in hallways, drawing-rooms and parlours. Electric lights to replace the rather hazardous traditional candles were first advertised in 1887, and a huge range of decorative glass baubles, stars, streamers, tiny musical instruments and colourful satin and velvet pouches of sweets and nuts was displayed on shop counters every December.

Poorer families could not afford to buy a tree, and many children only saw decorated trees at school or through the windows and doorways of other people's houses. Richard Church started at infant school just before Christmas and was overawed by the size of the tree and its decorations. 'My first day there was just before Christmas, so that at the start, I had the pill gilded by seeing the school-rooms decorated with paper-chains and tinsel stars.... All I recollect now of that first day at school is the scene of vastness: the enormous hall, the classrooms, the endless files of children constantly on the move; the big Christmas tree and the grey-haired figure standing by it, handing out gifts taken from its sugary twigs as another woman shouted numbers. The meaning of all this arithmetic escaped me; but I was aware of a firmness, a cold, impersonal pretence of

Crackers were popular for birthday parties as well as for Christmas.

benevolence in the air.... I found myself being pushed forward to the tree, and taking from the old lady a sugar pig. It had a pink-mauve snout, and a blue ribbon round its neck. Its hide sparkled, hard and crystalline.'

In large manor houses and stately homes, there was always a tall decorated tree and every year the children of the estate workers and sometimes other village children were invited to come and hear the carol singing round the tree and to receive a present. Vita Sackville-West describes in *The Edwardians* how the children of the head carpenter '... came annually to the Christmas tree, there to receive a toy, an apple and an orange....' Joan Poynder recalls: 'There was a huge Christmas tree and choirboys because we had a chapel. The choirboys came and sang carols... and all the staff were given presents and came and got them off the Christmas tree.'

Christmas Shopping

Shops and big stores were intriguing to a child at any time of the year, but at Christmas they became a fairyland of magic, full of special Christmassy things – shiny tinsely decorations to hang on the tree, crackers made from sparkling paper with promising little treats concealed within, special foods to tempt the shopper – raisins and figs, almonds and walnuts, chocolates and candies – Christmas cards with their bright colours and pretty pictures, toys and books and party frocks. Sonia Keppel looked forward to her Christmas

shopping trip with her mother with eager anticipation. 'Our Christmas walk down Oxford Street
was my annual delight. Everything seemed to
enhance our intimacy, the jostling crowds that
necessitated my clinging close to Mamma's arm,
the cold wind which made her hold one of my
hands in her muff, the brightly lit shops for us to
enjoy together.' Her favourite was obviously the
toy shop, and she would stand and gaze at the
array of dolls and brightly coloured playthings set
amongst strands of tinsel. 'Usually in the middle
of its window was a Christmas tree hung with
candles and crackers and toys, and surmounted by
a fairy doll wearing a tinsel crown, and holding a
wand with a star on it! All around the tree, the best
dolls were displayed in boxes, in beds, in perambulators!. . . . And together, Mamma and I would
view them, I with a delicious anticipatory thrill
that one of them might become mine. . . .'

Esther Stokes remembers that 'One of the
treats at Christmas was to be taken up to the
Haymarket stores to choose crackers. And each
one of us was allowed to choose a box. . . . They
were quite modest; we didn't have very elaborate
things at all.'

*Santa Claus could
always be relied
upon to produce
exciting toys from
his sack.*

Father Christmas

Father Christmas was a relatively recent addition to Christmas. In the 1870s, vague references were made to a benevolent character who visited on Christmas Eve, but neither Santa Claus nor Father Christmas really seems to have come to life until 1878, when a new image of him appeared descending chimneys and delivering presents into children's stockings. In the 1870s, Bon Marché in Liverpool introduced the first Christmas Fairyland, which became an annual event, and in the 1890s Santa was recruited to oversee the children's visits there. In 1885 he was seen in London distributing gifts in Fortnum and Mason and elsewhere, and in 1898, Old Father Christmas presided over the Monster Lucky Tub at Madame Tussaud's throughout the week following 25 December. By Edwardian times children were writing letters to Santa and longing for Christmas morning, when they could explore their stockings to see what the red-coated, white-bearded gentleman had brought them.

Here We Come A'Wassailing

Carol singing dates back to the twelfth century, but the custom almost died out in early Victorian days. In the 1860s the traditional songs were rediscovered and rescued by folk song collectors and again became an important part of the revelling. By the 1900s they were very popular and groups of singers would go round the village or neighbourhood singing their greetings to the residents and

One of the only times the children were allowed into the kitchen was to mix the Christmas pudding.

collecting money. A.L. Rowse writes: 'Carol singing at Christmas was the greatest pleasure of all, and the most profitable. We were paid some three or four shillings a quarter in the choir, in accordance with our attendance. . . . We looked forward to Christmas as our chief opportunity of making money on a more generous scale. Besides this, it was very exciting in itself. The boys went round in two different bands, seniors and juniors. . . . In the first Christmas we made about 3s 6d each. . . . We ended up the Christmas tired and pleased with hoarse throats, but plenty of oranges, dates, chocolates and sweets.'

Christmas Morning At Last

The opening of the stocking was the most thrilling part of the season's celebrations. Cynthia Asquith, recalling '. . . that dazzling climax up to which the entire slowly revolving year seemed to lead,' describes her and her brother's pleasure at discovering one surprise after another: 'Brilliantly vivid, the morning of my last nursery Christmas returns to me. Waking at a preposterously early hour, I shook Colin out of his deep sleep to share the thrill of the first tentative probings of the bulges in our heavily weighted stockings, before, full of wild surmise, we dragged out the rustling parcels, and fumbled with knotted string and crackling paper until our cots were heaped high with the litter of unpacking. . . . I can still see Colin sitting upright in his cot, his eyes ablaze, his cheeks flushed, and then tearing all over the house prattling of his new playthings and wishing everyone a happy Christmas.'

For Rachel Ferguson the morning came as a relief: 'I shall always remember the waking up on Christmas morning; realizing that the endless night was over, and feeling in that grey half-light with a sensation of justified piracy the swollen stocking full of rustling bulges.' And Leonard Clark remembers a sense of disbelief: 'Was it really Christmas morning? And there, hanging like a dislocated black limb, was my stocking at the bottom of the bed. So he had not forgotten me. But his coming and his kindness were as much a mystery as ever. Who had told him I wanted *Treasure Island* and what would my mother have said if she had seen the way he had stretched my stocking? The apple and orange, whose cold faces I warmed against my night-gown, I had half expected. But would the knife have that thing for getting out the stones in horses' hooves?'

After stockings came breakfast and then off to the traditional church service. 'The recollection of those Christmas Day breakfasts has long ago departed,' writes Leonard Clark, 'but I suppose they were just the same kind of breakfasts which were being enjoyed at a thousand other tables on that particular morning. However, I can remember the red jersey which Mother had knitted for me, the gaudily decorated tin of London hum-bugs which my brother gave to me. . . .' As he and his family arrived at church, 'The whole building seemed like a forest; there was so much holly about that even members of the congregation seemed to be sprouting it. . . . The vicar, white-bearded like an Old Testament patriarch, smiled on his flock, and we, the twelve devils and angels of the choir, lifted up our voices and sang Hark the Herald Angels Sing. . . .'

CHRISTMAS·MORNING
WHY, SANTA CLAUS IS KIND, INDEED!
WE NEVER WROTE A LETTER.

An early 20th-century Christmas card showing a typical happy scene on Christmas morning.

Roast Turkey and Christmas Pudding

Memories of presents and church services are all mixed up with recollections of turkey dinners and sixpences hidden in Christmas pudding. Henry Vigne's memory is fairly typical: 'We went to church on Christmas morning and we had an enormous meal. And I think we were driven out or I used to go for a walk in the afternoon, probably on the excuse that the dogs had to have exercise …. We played charades and … possibly some neighbours came in.' For Florence Atherton, 'Christmas Day was the happiest day of the year. And Mother always made a big Christmas pudding and a nice dinner, turkey and everything else, and my father used to come out with the Christmas spirit and we used to have a branch of holly and he used to have a little drop of brandy in

the glass and he used to set fire to the holly and pour the brandy over it.' Katherine Chorley always seemed to get the sixpence in her pudding: 'When the moment for plum pudding arrived, for several years the laughter turned on me because wasn't it extraordinary that I always got the sixpence! The year that I discovered Louisa inserting it surreptitiously into my helping as she handed me my plate was a major landmark on the road to an adult outlook.'

Children who normally ate all their meals in the nursery with Nanny were often allowed to join the rest of the family for Christmas dinner or luncheon. Sonia Keppel's family ate together: 'On Christmas Day, the children had luncheon in the dining-room. Confronted by a mass of knives and forks and glasses, I felt like a juggler without his skill. The food was disguised beyond all hope of

recognition. And each year my sense of panic returned as the footmen shut the shutters and plunged the dining-room into darkness before the flaming plum pudding appeared.'

Working-class children did not enjoy such luxury and sumptuousness. Usually there was not even a pudding on the table, let alone the brandy to make it flame. Working Men's Clubs and charitable organizations often laid on parties for the poorer children. Speaking of the general activities of the clubs, Arthur Newton remembers that 'Children's Christmas parties and outings were also a feature of the clubs. For weeks before an event, small collections and raffles were promoted to get enough funds to pay for the kiddies' "do". A Christmas party was indeed a boisterous affair. Imagine a couple of hundred youngsters after feeding themselves on bread and jam, cakes and lemonade, yelling themselves hoarse at the antics of a Punch and Judy show, or some red-nosed clown or comic on the club's stage.'

Thomas Morgan, whose family was quite poor, says: 'We got a bit of a joint, we used to have a roast, done in front of the fire on what they called a Dutch oven. . . . Christmas Day we used to go in the pub – 'cause children were allowed in the pubs then and we used to play on the floor in the sawdust. . . . I don't suppose we was ever at home at Christmas time. We all went to a Christmas party at some mission . . . that was the usual thing for all poor kids then.' Thomas remembers that at those parties 'We used to sing a few hymns and

they used to have a magic lantern show, "Twinkle, twinkle little star", or something. Then, they'd show us a few pictures of different lands, you know, and after that they used to say, "Well come and have the cocoa" and buns and biscuits. . . . When we were at Shaftesbury Hall in Trinity Street, Borough, we used to get a proper Christmas dinner. . . . We used to get turkey – 'cause you could buy turkeys five shillings each then.'

In poorer rural communities, Christmas was a very simple affair. Things did not change very much from the 1890s of Flora Thompson's Lark Rise. 'Christmas Day passed very quietly. The men had a holiday from work and the children from school and the churchgoers attended special Christmas services. Mothers who had young children would buy them an orange each and a handful of nuts; but except at the end house and the inn, there was no hanging up of stockings, and those who had no kind elder sister or aunt in service to sent them parcels got no Christmas presents. Still, they did manage to make a little festival of it. Every year the farmer killed an ox for the purpose and gave each of his men a joint of beef, which duly appeared on the Christmas dinner-table together with plum pudding – not Christmas pudding, but suet duff with a good sprinkling of raisins. . . .'

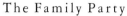

The Family Party

Rich families in high society celebrated the season with elaborate parties, and Sonia Keppel recalls spending the Christmases of her early childhood in the houses of various lords and ladies, friends of her parents. At the age of three she found herself at the home of Lord and Lady Howe, '... where I have no recollection of anything except an enormous grown-up fancy dress dinner-party on Christmas Eve. To this I was brought down dressed up as an admiral of the Fleet ....'

Katharine Chorley's family played games to amuse all age groups. 'General Knowledge was another Christmas game, and even Mother joined in this. Everyone had a piece of paper and you had to write down a list of subjects such as flower, mountain, battle, statesman, poet and so forth. Then someone picked a letter at random and in ten minutes of hectic private research into a well- or ill-stored mind you had to find an example of each subject beginning with the chosen letter.... Sometimes after I had gone to bed there would be music and I would lie awake listening whilst Mother sang to Auntie May's accompaniment.... Christmas was certainly the feast of family reunion, and every year the party reassembled, the bags of golf-clubs were stacked in the lobby, the housemaid scuttered along the gallery with hot-water cans at dressing-for-dinner time, the mistletoe hung over the stairs tied to a gallery baluster, Grundy saved a magnificent show of curly, Japanese crysanthemums to decorate the hall, and I

was allowed to join more and more freely in the grown-up fun. There was no break until 1914, and then the curtain rang down ....'

At these gatherings the assembled company played Charades, Postman's Knock, Musical Chairs, Sardines, Hunt the Thimble, Blind Man's Buff and Follow My Leader, Singing games included 'Here We Go Round the Mulberry Bush', 'Ring-a-Ring of Roses' and 'The Farmer's In His Dell'. There were quieter games of general knowledge and story-telling and sporting fun with Battledore and Shuttlecock, Ping-Pong and the Feather Game, in which the players had to keep a feather in the air for as long as possible by blowing it upwards. By the time the party was over, everyone was tired out after such an exciting day filled with good things to eat, presents, stockings full of gifts from Santa Claus and the exuberance and fun of the evening's games. Children went sleepily to bed, sad that Christmas Day was over for another year and that they would have to wait for an eternity of three hundred and sixty-four days before the next one.

Boxing Day

The Bank Holiday Act of 1871 extended Christmas to include Boxing Day, and by 1900, Boxing Day holidays for shops, banks and offices were usual in England and Wales (in Scotland it was 1 January that was the statutory holiday). So, Boxing Day was devoted to parties and sports and visiting the poor of the neighbourhood to offer food and gifts. For the aristocratic families it was also a day for hunting, and riders would assemble outside the main house for a hunt breakfast and stirrup cup before setting off across the fields. Children wrapped up in warm clothes and went off to build snowmen and slide toboggans down snowy slopes or skate on frozen ponds and lakes.

The Christmas Pantomime

By the 1830s and 40s, pantomimes had become purely Christmas events. In those days the harlequinade was the central part of the show, acquiring around it a mixture of song and dance, comic turns and acrobats. The harlequin element disappeared in the 1860s, leaving a show based usually on nursery themes and comedy. 'We went to the pantomime too, at Christmas,' Diana Cooper recalled, 'to see Dan Leno and Herbert Campbell as very old *Babes in the Wood*, and fairies invisibly wired on tiptoe for flights through transformation gauzes.' The shows often lasted for up to four hours and children were transfixed by the costumes and lights and scenes in which marching figures made complicated patterns of colour up and down the stage.

Sybil Pearce saw her local pantomime, which ran for a week during January. 'On the dress rehearsal nights we children would be given tickets to go to see the play of the current season, accompanied by the servants and nannies of our respective families.'

Some families went not to pantomimes but to plays and musicals. Gervas Huxley writes: 'The highlight of the Christmas holidays was the evening when my Godfather, Dighton Pollock, took me out to see the latest musical comedy at Daly's.' And in some homes amateur dramatics provided family entertainment.

And so the celebrations ended, and soon it was time to slip back into the routine of lessons and homework, playtimes with favourite teddies and train sets, mealtimes with Nanny's strict tuition in manners, walks to the local park, and occasional treats and outings to provide lighter moments. But the events of 1914 changed the face of Britain, and the golden days of Edwardian childhood were lost for ever.

BIBLIOGRAPHY

Every attempt has been made to contact the copyright holders to reproduce the following material:

References

Asquith, Cynthia, *Haply I May Remember*, James Barrie 1950

Barrie, J.M., *Peter Pan*, Hodder and Stoughton 1911

Beeton, Isabella, *Book of Household Management*, 1861

Betjeman, John, *Summoned by Bells*, John Murray, 1960

Blair, Anna, *Tea at Miss Cranston's*, Shepherd Walwyn 1985 (includes accounts by Anna Blair, Marie Condie and David Marriot)

Brazil, Angela, *The Fortunes of Philippa*, Blackie and Sons Ltd 1906

Brittain, Vera, *Testament of Youth*, Gollancz 1933

Brooke, Jocelyn, *The Dog at Clambercrown*, Bodley Head 1955

Cardus, Neville, *Autobiography*, Collins 1947

Chorley, Katharine, *Manchester Made Them*, Faber and Faber 1950

Church, Richard, *Over The Bridge*, Heinemann 1955, courtesy of the Estate of Richard Church

Clark, Leonard, *Greenwood: A Gloucester Childhood*, Max Parish and Co Ltd

Codrington, Kenneth de Burgh, *Cricket in the Grass*, Faber and Faber 1959

Cooper, Diana, *The Rainbow Comes and Goes*, Rupert Hart-Davis 1958

Cooper, Duff, *Old Men Forget*, Rupert Hart-Davis 1953

Cowles, Virginia, *Edward VII and His Circle*, Hamish Hamilton 1956

Ferguson, Rachel, *We Were Amused*, Cape 1958, courtesy of Campbell Thomson & McLaughlin Ltd

Ferguson, Ruby, *Children At The Shop*, Hodder and Stoughton 1967

Garnett, David, *The Golden Echo*, Chatto and Windus 1953, courtesy of A.P. Watt as the Executors of the Estate of David Garnett

Gill, Arthur Eric, *Autobiography*, Cape 1940

Green, Henry, *Pack My Bag*, Hogarth 1940

Greenwood, Walter, *There Was a Time*, Jonathan Cape 1967

Huxley, Gervas, *Both Hands*, Chatto and Windus 1970

Keppel, Sonia, *Edwardian Daughter*, Hamish Hamilton 1958

Kipling, Rudyard, *The Brushwood Boy*, Scribner's Sons 1936; *Puck of Pook's Hill*, Scribner's Sons 1909

Lehmann, Rosamond, *The Swan in the Evening: Fragments of an Inner Life*, Collins 1967, courtesy of The Society of Authors

Lewis, C. Day, *The Buried Day*, Chatto and Windus 1960, courtesy of the Estate of C. Day Lewis

Lewis, C.S., *Surprised By Joy*, Geoffrey Bles 1958

London, Jack, *People of the Abyss*, Macmillan 1903

Lynch, Patricia, *A Storyteller's Childhood*, Dent 1947

Pope, W. MacQueen, *Give Me Yesterday*, Hutchinson 1957

Newton, Arthur, *Years of Change*, Hackney Workers Educational Association Enterprise Publications 1974

Pearce, Sybil, *Edwardian Childhood in Bedford Park*, Published by the author 1977

Priestley, J.B., *The Edwardians*, Heinemann/Rainbird 1970

Potter, Stephen, *Steps to Immaturity*, Rupert Hart-Davis 1959

Raverat, Gwen, *A Cambridgeshire Childhood*, Faber and Faber 1952

Read, Sir Herbert, *Annals of Innocence and Experience*, Faber and Faber 1940

Rowse, A.L., *A Cornish Childhood*, Anthony Mott Ltd 1982

Sackville-West, Vita, *The Edwardians*, Penguin 1935

Stark, Freya, *Traveller's Prelude*, Murray 1950

Thompson, Flora, *Lark Rise to Candleford*, OUP 1939

Thompson, Thea, *Edwardian Childhoods*, Routledge and Kegan Paul 1981, reprinted by permission of the Peters Fraser & Dunlop Group Ltd (includes accounts by Florence Atherton, Geoffrey Brady, Clifford Hills, Thomas Morgan, Joan Poynder, Esther Stokes, Henry Vigne, Annie Wilson and Jack York.)

Waugh, Evelyn, *Brideshead Revisited*, Chapman and Hall 1945

Wright, Mary, *Cornish Treats*, Alison Hodge 1986

Further reading

The following books were particularly useful in my research:

Ashdown, Dulcie M., *Christmas Past*, Elm Tree Books 1976

Beckett, Jane and Cherry, Deborah, *The Edwardian Era*, Phaidon and Barbican Art gallery 1987

Briggs, Asa, *They Saw It Happen*, Basil Blackwell 1960

Cecil, Robert, *Life in Edwardian England*, Batsford 1969

Cooper, E.H., *The Twentieth Century Child*, John Lane 1905

Foot, P.W.R., *The Child in the Twentieth Century*, Cassell 1968

Hardy, Jonathan Gathorne, *The Rise and Fall of the British Nanny*, Weidenfeld and Nicolson 1985

Laver, James, *Edwardian Promenade*, Edward Hulton 1958

Opie, Peter, *Children's Games in Street and Playground*, Oxford University Press 1984

Priestley J.B., *The Edwardians*, Heinemann 1970

Read, Donald, *Edwardian England*, Harrap 1972

Scout Association, *75 Years of Scouting*, Scout Association 1982

Smith, Joanna, *Edwardian Children*, Hutchinson 1983

Stevenson, Pauline, *Edwardian Fashion*, Ian Allan 1980

Thompson, Paul, *The Edwardians*, Weidenfeld and Nicolson 1975

INDEX

Picture credits

Every attempt has been made to contact the copyright holders to reproduce the material from the following sources:

Bodleian Library, Oxford (John Johnson Collection): p. 28, 32, 79, 83, 85, 93, 99, 123 and all the children's 'scraps' throughout the book.

Bridgeman Art Library: title page, Le Mair H. Willebeck; p. 6 Randolph Caldecott, Christopher Wood Gallery; 21, 27 Kate Greenaway; 31 John Strickland Goodall, Christopher Wood Gallery; 90 Joseph Kirkpatrick; 94 Richard Doyle; 107, 108 Chris Roger Church Collection; 111 Mrs Hillier; 118, John L. Byam-Shaw, Christopher Wood Gallery; 134 Dame Laura Knight, Laing Art Gallery; 138 John Strickland Goodall, Christopher Wood Gallery; 142 Paul Emile Lecomte, Galerie George; 151 Karl Rogers, Trustees of the V & A; 154. Cover picture Peter Szumouski; painted tin toys, Museum of London.

Mary Evans Picture Library: p. 7, 9, 11, 12, 13, 16, 17, 22, 29, 30, 45, 46, 49, 51, 52, 53, 57, 60, 63, 64, 65, 69, 71, 76, 81, 87, 88, 92, 95, 96, 99, 101, 103, 104, 106, 112, 120, 126, 128, 130, 136, 140, 147.

Fine Art Photographs and Library Ltd: p. 10 Harry Brooker; 19 Paul Fischer; 23 Charles Goldsburgh Anderson; 26 William Mainwaring Palin; 35 A.E. Backner, Gavin Graham Gallery; 38 Buddig Anwylini Pughe; 42 Percy Tarrant; 55 Dorothy Fitchew; 59 Percy Tarrant; 62 James Hayllar; 67 Charles Edward Wilson; 75 Harry Brooker; 78 Carlton Alfred Smith; 82 Sarah Magregor; 91 Charles Edward Wilson; 102 Arthur John Elsley; 119 Jane M. Dealy; 122 Hector Caffieri; 131 Myles Birket Foster; 143 E. Lance; 146 Percy Tarrant.

Illustrated London News: p. 8, 152.

National Motor Museum: p. 61

National Museum of Photography, Film and Television: p. 100.

The Robert Opie Collection: p. 37, 39, 40, 50, 89, 135, 150.

Pollock's Toy Museum: p. 114

The Royal Photographic Society, Bath: p. 33 Ernest G. Boon; 109, 117 Mathilde Weil; 137 Horace Nicholls.